Software Development:
A Career Guide

Software Development:
A Career Guide

Marc Thatcher

MURPHY & MOORE
www.murphy-moorepublishing.com

Software Development: A Career Guide
Marc Thatcher
ISBN: 978-1-63987-808-6 (Hardback)

⊛MURPHY & MOORE

Murphy & Moore Publishing
1 Rockefeller Plaza,
New York City,
NY 10020, USA

Cataloging-in-Publication Data

Software development : a career guide / Marc Thatcher.
     p. cm.
Includes bibliographical references and index.
ISBN 978-1-63987-808-6
1. Computer software--Development--Vocational guidance. 2. Computer programmers--Vocational guidance.
I. Thatcher, Marc.
QA76.76.D47 S64 2023
005.1--dc23

Table of Contents

Permissions

Index

Preface

Software is typically developed to meet the demands of potential customers, clients and businesses or for personal use. Software development refers to the process of designing, programming, conceiving, testing, documenting and bug fixing which are inherent processes involved in the creation and maintenance of software components. Writing and managing the source code is an important aspect of software development. Software products are developed through meticulous research, prototyping, reuse, re-engineering, etc. Some of the many roles involved in this functional domain are computer programmers, software developers, software engineers, consulting software engineers and software publishers, among many others. This textbook provides comprehensive insights into the field of software development. Most of the topics introduced herein discuss the various careers involved in this domain and the ways to succeed in them. It is an essential guide for both academicians and those who wish to pursue this discipline further.

A detailed account of the significant topics covered in this book is provided below:

Chapter 1- The process by which software applications, frameworks and components are designed, programmed, documented, tested and perfected is known as software development. It involves writing the source code and maintaining it. This chapter explores the vital aspects of software development and software development life cycle.

Chapter 2- The process involved in solving a problem or a set of problems and planning a software solution is known as software design. It involves planning a software solution and problem solving. The high level structures of a software system and the process of creating such systems and structures is known as software architecture. This chapter has been carefully written to describe the key aspects of software design and software architecture and describes the job prospects of a software designer and a software architect.

Chapter 3- Software development encompasses the development of a wide range of software operating systems, business applications, games, computer applications and network control systems. This allows specializations in a number of fields. Some of the professionals working in this domain are software analysts, software managers, software developers and programmers, consultants, software engineers, etc. This chapter has been carefully written to provide an overview of such software development careers and the ways to become successful professionals in these domains.

Chapter 4- Software testing is the investigation of the quality of a product for determining its suitability for use and detecting software bugs, if any. This chapter explores some of the fundamental aspects of software testing and includes topics such as testing antivirus and security software, performing software product testing, categorizing software defects, using static analysis testing, etc.

Chapter 5- Software maintenance refers to the process by which a software product is modified and refined to correct faults and improve performance. The topics elucidated in this chapter address some of the techniques of software maintenance such as for improving software quality, fixing bugs, managing a new software implementation, finding XPath using Firebug, etc.

It gives me an immense pleasure to thank our entire team for their efforts. Finally in the end, I would like to thank my family and colleagues who have been a great source of inspiration and support.

Marc Thatcher

CHAPTER 1

Software Development: An Introduction

The process by which software applications, frameworks and components are designed, programmed, documented, tested and perfected is known as software development. It involves writing the source code and maintaining it. This chapter provides an introduction to software development and explores the fundamental aspects of software development and software development life cycle.

Software development is the process by which a company, team, or individual devises and implements an overall plan to create a new software program. This process can also be applied to an established program to create a new version of that software, though this is usually an abridged version of the process unless the new version is largely different from the previous one. Numerous steps are involved in this process, beginning with understanding what is needed from software, developing a plan for creating it, writing the code, and bug testing prior to launch. Software development can be a process that involves anything from a single programmer to dozens or hundreds of individuals.

The process of developing software usually begins with research or a general understanding of what type of software is needed in the marketplace. This may be an entirely new program that addresses an unfulfilled need or a new piece of software in an existing market. As development begins, this research establishes the purpose of the software being developed and the overall goals of the development.

Once those involved in software development have a goal for the program they are working on, they can begin developing the plan for implementing that software. A great deal of work is typically required before any actual code is created, especially for aspects of a program such as the user interface and the basic architecture. Graphic designers, interface developers, programmers, and producers on a large team can all be involved in this stage of development.

Software development then typically moves from these early phases of brainstorming ideas for creating the overall structure of the program to actually writing the code for the software. This implementation typically involves one or more computer programmers, and the source code is created in any number of different applications, programming languages, and other utilities. During and after the code has been created, a great deal of testing is typically involved to ensure the program runs properly and is as free of bugs, glitches, and errors as possible.

Ongoing software development may continue even once a program is written, tested, and launched to the general public. Such development may serve to fix errors found after launch or introduce minor improvements and some new features. User feedback can also be utilized to gather information for ways in which the program might be improved in a larger sense. This feedback can then be used to begin software development again on a new version of the program, which can offer features and utilities not found in the previous version.

Software Development Life Cycle

Software Development Life Cycle, SDLC for short, is a well-defined, structured sequence of stages in software engineering to develop the intended software product.

SDLC Activities

SDLC provides a series of steps to be followed to design and develop a software product efficiently. SDLC framework includes the following steps:

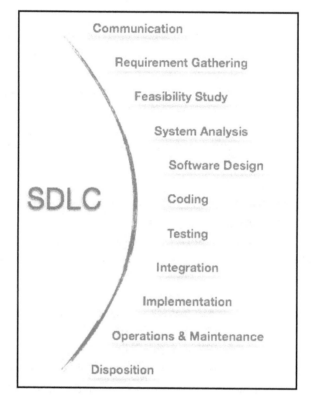

Communication

This is the first step where the user initiates the request for a desired software product. He contacts the service provider and tries to negotiate the terms. He submits his request to the service providing organization in writing.

Requirement Gathering

This step onwards the software development team works to carry on the project. The team holds discussions with various stakeholders from problem domain and tries to bring out as much information as possible on their requirements. The requirements are contemplated and segregated into user requirements, system requirements and functional requirements. The requirements are collected using a number of practices as given -

- Studying the existing or obsolete system and software,

- Conducting interviews of users and developers,
- Referring to the database or
- Collecting answers from the questionnaires.

Feasibility Study

After requirement gathering, the team comes up with a rough plan of software process. At this step the team analyzes if a software can be made to fulfill all requirements of the user and if there is any possibility of software being no more useful. It is found out, if the project is financially, practically and technologically feasible for the organization to take up. There are many algorithms available, which help the developers to conclude the feasibility of a software project.

System Analysis

At this step the developers decide a roadmap of their plan and try to bring up the best software model suitable for the project. System analysis includes Understanding of software product limitations, learning system related problems or changes to be done in existing systems beforehand, identifying and addressing the impact of project on organization and personnel etc. The project team analyzes the scope of the project and plans the schedule and resources accordingly.

Software Design

Next step is to bring down whole knowledge of requirements and analysis on the desk and design the software product. The inputs from users and information gathered in requirement gathering phase are the inputs of this step. The output of this step comes in the form of two designs; logical design and physical design. Engineers produce meta-data and data dictionaries, logical diagrams, data-flow diagrams and in some cases pseudo codes.

Coding

This step is also known as programming phase. The implementation of software design starts in terms of writing program code in the suitable programming language and developing error-free executable programs efficiently.

Testing

An estimate says that 50% of whole software development process should be tested. Errors may ruin the software from critical level to its own removal. Software testing is done while coding by the developers and thorough testing is conducted by testing experts at various levels of code such as module testing, program testing, product testing, in-house testing and testing the product at user's end. Early discovery of errors and their remedy is the key to reliable software.

Integration

Software may need to be integrated with the libraries, databases and other program(s). This stage of SDLC is involved in the integration of software with outer world entities.

Implementation

This means installing the software on user machines. At times, software needs post-installation configurations at user end. Software is tested for portability and adaptability and integration related issues are solved during implementation.

Operation and Maintenance

This phase confirms the software operation in terms of more efficiency and less errors. If required, the users are trained on, or aided with the documentation on how to operate the software and how to keep the software operational. The software is maintained timely by updating the code according to the changes taking place in user end environment or technology. This phase may face challenges from hidden bugs and real-world unidentified problems.

Disposition

As time elapses, the software may decline on the performance front. It may go completely obsolete or may need intense upgradation. Hence a pressing need to eliminate a major portion of the system arises. This phase includes archiving data and required software components, closing down the system, planning disposition activity and terminating system at appropriate end-of-system time.

CHAPTER 2

Software Design and Architechure

The process involved in solving a problem or a set of problems and planning a software solution is known as software design. It involves planning a software solution and problem solving. The high level structures of a software system and the process of creating such systems and structures is known as software architecture. This chapter has been carefully written to describe the key aspects of software design and software architecture and describes the job prospects of a software designer and a software architect.

Software Design

Software design is a process to transform user requirements into some suitable form, which helps the programmer in software coding and implementation.

For assessing user requirements, an SRS (Software Requirement Specification) document is created whereas for coding and implementation, there is a need of more specific and detailed requirements in software terms. The output of this process can directly be used into implementation in programming languages.

Software design is the first step in SDLC (Software Design Life Cycle), which moves the concentration from problem domain to solution domain. It tries to specify how to fulfill the requirements mentioned in SRS.

Software Design Levels

Software design yields three levels of results:

- Architectural Design - The architectural design is the highest abstract version of the system. It identifies the software as a system with many components interacting with each other. At this level, the designers get the idea of proposed solution domain.

- High-level Design- The high-level design breaks the 'single entity-multiple component' concept of architectural design into less-abstracted view of sub-systems and modules and depicts their interaction with each other. High-level design focuses on how the system along with all of its components can be implemented in forms of modules. It recognizes modular structure of each sub-system and their relation and interaction among each other.

- Detailed Design- Detailed design deals with the implementation part of what is seen as a system and its sub-systems in the previous two designs. It is more detailed towards modules and their implementations. It defines logical structure of each module and their interfaces to communicate with other modules.

Modularization

Modularization is a technique to divide a software system into multiple discrete and independent modules, which are expected to be capable of carrying out task(s) independently. These modules may work as basic constructs for the entire software. Designers tend to design modules such that they can be executed and/or compiled separately and independently.

Modular design unintentionally follows the rules of 'divide and conquer' problem-solving strategy this is because there are many other benefits attached with the modular design of a software.

Advantage of modularization:

- Smaller components are easier to maintain
- Program can be divided based on functional aspects
- Desired level of abstraction can be brought in the program
- Components with high cohesion can be re-used again
- Concurrent execution can be made possible
- Desired from security aspect.

Concurrency

Back in time, all software are meant to be executed sequentially. By sequential execution we mean that the coded instruction will be executed one after another implying only one portion of program being activated at any given time. Say, a software has multiple modules, then only one of all the modules can be found active at any time of execution.

In software design, concurrency is implemented by splitting the software into multiple independent units of execution, like modules and executing them in parallel. In other words, concurrency provides capability to the software to execute more than one part of code in parallel to each other.

It is necessary for the programmers and designers to recognize those modules, which can be made parallel execution.

Example

The spell check feature in word processor is a module of software, which runs along side the word processor itself.

Coupling and Cohesion

When a software program is modularized, its tasks are divided into several modules based on some characteristics. As we know, modules are set of instructions put together in order to achieve some tasks. They are though, considered as single entity but may refer to each other to work together. There are measures by which the quality of a design of modules and their interaction among them can be measured. These measures are called coupling and cohesion.

Cohesion

Cohesion is a measure that defines the degree of intra-dependability within elements of a module. The greater the cohesion, the better is the program design.

There are seven types of cohesion, namely –

- Co-incidental cohesion - It is unplanned and random cohesion, which might be the result of breaking the program into smaller modules for the sake of modularization. Because it is unplanned, it may serve confusion to the programmers and is generally not-accepted.

- Logical cohesion - When logically categorized elements are put together into a module, it is called logical cohesion.

- Temporal Cohesion - When elements of module are organized such that they are processed at a similar point in time, it is called temporal cohesion.

- Procedural cohesion - When elements of module are grouped together, which are executed sequentially in order to perform a task, it is called procedural cohesion.

- Communicational cohesion - When elements of module are grouped together, which are executed sequentially and work on same data (information), it is called communicational cohesion.

- Sequential cohesion - When elements of module are grouped because the output of one element serves as input to another and so on, it is called sequential cohesion.

- Functional cohesion - It is considered to be the highest degree of cohesion, and it is highly expected. Elements of module in functional cohesion are grouped because they all contribute to a single well-defined function. It can also be reused.

Coupling

Coupling is a measure that defines the level of inter-dependability among modules of a program. It tells at what level the modules interfere and interact with each other. The lower the coupling, the better the program.

There are five levels of coupling, namely -

- Content coupling - When a module can directly access or modify or refer to the content of another module, it is called content level coupling.

- Common coupling- When multiple modules have read and write access to some global data, it is called common or global coupling.

- Control coupling- Two modules are called control-coupled if one of them decides the function of the other module or changes its flow of execution.

- Stamp coupling- When multiple modules share common data structure and work on different part of it, it is called stamp coupling.

- Data coupling- Data coupling is when two modules interact with each other by means of passing data (as parameter). If a module passes data structure as parameter, then the receiving module should use all its components.

Ideally, no coupling is considered to be the best.

Design Verification

The output of software design process is design documentation, pseudo codes, detailed logic diagrams, process diagrams, and detailed description of all functional or non-functional requirements.

The next phase, which is the implementation of software, depends on all outputs mentioned above.

It is then becomes necessary to verify the output before proceeding to the next phase. The early any mistake is detected, the better it is or it might not be detected until testing of the product. If the outputs of design phase are in formal notation form, then their associated tools for verification should be used otherwise a thorough design review can be used for verification and validation.

By structured verification approach, reviewers can detect defects that might be caused by overlooking some conditions. A good design review is important for good software design, accuracy and quality.

The stages of software design include applying and putting into practice everything we have learnt from the Blueprint, such as:

- Contextual Research – designing the right interface requires a deep understanding of your audience, such as visual aesthetics, clarity of design and colour tones to ensure ease of use.

- User Interface Concept Design – creating a minimum of 3 different visual styles, incorporating all design elements including buttons, navigation, visual notifications and call to actions (to name a few) .

- Accessibility Considerations – basing our design ethos on the idea that anyone could use with ease, without being tech savvy.

- Scalability and Security – designing all systems to be scalable and secure, maintaining a stable level of performance whilst protecting users and data as the system expands.

- Development Framework and Cycle – using a proven development framework and tools to build the software we design. We operate Agile methodologies using the proven JIRA software management tool.

- Change Management – allowing for inevitable change in the design eases delays in development, particularly on longer projects. Our planning and processes allow plenty of flexibility in-flight without causing major impacts to time or budget.

- Platform – designing applications for the most current web and mobile platforms, based on technology people are using today.

- Cost – incorporating the most effective design to maximise the value, impact and longevity of the software application. We hand pick talent that have a deep understanding of both design and development – this lends to cost effective design decisions early on.

Job Areas of Software Designer

While there are many different types of software designer jobs available, many of them can be classified within a few basic categories. Systems engineer positions usually involve software designers who are responsible for developing and overseeing computer systems for a particular company. Application engineers are software designers responsible for creating new computer software, utilities, and applications, often by creating and testing code for a new software program throughout the development process. There are also a number of software designer jobs within certain specialized fields, such as game development, website creation and administration, and within specific aspects of software development such as user interface (UI) design.

Software designer jobs can cover a wide range of fields and processes, depending on the type of software a designer wants to develop. Many of these jobs require a systems engineer, who is a software designer responsible for the development and oversight of software and computer systems within a company. A retail company, for example, might use a basic commercial software program to track sales and record budgets for the company. Some companies, however, have software designer jobs available for someone who creates new software for the company to use, customized to meet the particular needs of that company and developed and overseen by the designer.

There are also software designer jobs for designers interested in creating new software programs at a software company, often called application engineers. These designers create code for a new program, using a design document to guide the development of the software. This development process usually goes through multiple steps as additional utilities and features are added to the core software. Many of these companies also have software designer jobs for testers, who use the software in an effort to find bugs and errors that need to be fixed prior to commercial release of a program.

Many software designer jobs are similar to application engineering, but are oriented to a particular industry within software development or one facet of such development. Programmers within the game industry, for example, are typically software designers with an interest in developing software for gaming, often including artificial intelligence (AI) programming and other aspects of game development. There are also designers who focus on a particular aspect of development and choose to specialize in that area. Software designer jobs for these individuals can be found in specialized fields such as UI design and development, which requires an understanding of how people interface and interact with technology.

Software Architecture

Software architecture refers to the high level structures of a software system and the discipline of creating such structures and systems. Each structure comprises software elements, relations among them, and properties of both elements and relations. The *architecture* of a software system is a metaphor, analogous to the architecture of a building. It functions as a blueprint for the system and the developing project, laying out the tasks necessary to be executed by the design teams.

Software architecture is about making fundamental structural choices which are costly to change once implemented. Software architecture choices include specific structural options from possibilities in the design of software. For example, the systems that controlled the space shuttle launch vehicle had the requirement of being very fast and very reliable. Therefore, an appropriate real-time computing language would need to be chosen. Additionally, to satisfy the need for reliability the choice could be made to have multiple redundant and independently produced copies of the program, and to run these copies on independent hardware while cross-checking results.

Documenting software architecture facilitates communication between stakeholders, captures early decisions about the high-level design, and allows reuse of design components between projects.

Scope

Opinions vary as to the scope of software architectures:

- Overall, macroscopic system structure; this refers to architecture as a higher level abstraction of a software system that consists of a collection of computational components together with connectors that describe the interaction between these components.

- The important stuff—whatever that is; this refers to the fact that software architects should concern themselves with those decisions that have high impact on the system and its stakeholders.

- That which is fundamental to understanding a system in its environment".

- Things that people perceive as hard to change; since designing the architecture takes place at the beginning of a software system's lifecycle, the architect should focus on decisions that "have to" be right the first time. Following this line of thought, architectural design issues may become non-architectural once their irreversibility can be overcome.

- A set of architectural design decisions; software architecture should not be considered merely a set of models or structures, but should include the decisions that lead to these particular structures, and the rationale behind them. This insight has led to substantial research into software architecture knowledge management.

There is no sharp distinction between software architecture versus design and requirements engineering. They are all part of a "chain of intentionality" from high-level intentions to low-level details.

Software Architecture Topics

Software Architecture Description

Software architecture description involves the principles and practices of modeling and representing architectures, using mechanisms such as: architecture description languages, architecture viewpoints, and architecture frameworks.

Architecture Description Languages

An architecture description language (ADL) is any means of expression used to describe a software architecture (ISO/IEC/IEEE 42010). Many special-purpose ADLs have been developed since the 1990s, including AADL (SAE standard), Wright (developed by Carnegie Mellon), Acme (developed by Carnegie Mellon), xADL (developed by UCI), Darwin (developed by Imperial College London), DAOP-ADL (developed by University of Málaga), SBC-ADL (developed by National Sun Yat-Sen University), and ByADL (University of L'Aquila, Italy).

Architecture Viewpoints

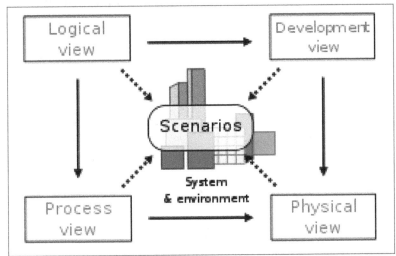

4+1 Architectural View Model.

Software architecture descriptions are commonly organized into views, which are analogous to the different types of blueprints made in building architecture. Each view addresses a set of system concerns, following the conventions of its *viewpoint*, where a viewpoint is a specification that describes the notations, modeling, and analysis techniques to use in a view that express the architecture in question from the perspective of a given set of stakeholders and their concerns. The viewpoint specifies not only the concerns framed (i.e., to be addressed) but the presentation, model kinds used, conventions used and any consistency (correspondence) rules to keep a view consistent with other views.

Architecture Frameworks

An architecture framework captures the "conventions, principles and practices for the description of architectures established within a specific domain of application and/or community of stakeholders". A framework is usually implemented in terms of one or more viewpoints or ADLs.

Architectural Styles and Patterns

An architectural pattern is a general, reusable solution to a commonly occurring problem in software architecture within a given context. Architectural patterns are often documented as software design patterns.

Following traditional building architecture, a 'software architectural style' is a specific method of construction, characterized by the features that make it notable" (architectural style).

> *"An architectural style defines: a family of systems in terms of a pattern of structural organization; a vocabulary of components and connectors, with constraints on how they can be combined."*

> *"Architectural styles are reusable 'packages' of design decisions and constraints that are applied to an architecture to induce chosen desirable qualities."*

There are many recognized architectural patterns and styles, among them:

- Blackboard
- Client-server (2-tier, 3-tier, n-tier, cloud computing exhibit this style)
- Component-based
- Data-centric
- Event-driven (or implicit invocation)
- Layered (or multilayered architecture)
- Microservices architecture
- Monolithic application
- Peer-to-peer (P2P)
- Pipes and filters
- Plug-ins
- Representational state transfer (REST)
- Rule-based
- Service-oriented
- Shared nothing architecture
- Space-based architecture

Some treat architectural patterns and architectural styles as the same, some treat styles as specializations of patterns. What they have in common is both patterns and styles are idioms for architects to use, they "provide a common language" or "vocabulary" with which to describe classes of systems.

Software Architecture and Agile Development

There are also concerns that software architecture leads to too much Big Design Up Front, especially among proponents of agile software development. A number of methods have been developed to balance the trade-offs of up-front design and agility, including the agile method DSDM which mandates a "Foundations" phase during which "just enough" architectural foundations are laid. IEEE Software devoted a special issue to the interaction between agility and architecture.

Software Architecture Erosion

Software architecture erosion (or "decay") refers to the gap observed between the planned and actual architecture of a software system as realized in its implementation. Software architecture erosion occurs when implementation decisions either do not fully achieve the architecture-as-planned or otherwise violate constraints or principles of that architecture. The gap between planned and actual architectures is sometimes understood in terms of the notion of technical debt.

As an example, consider a strictly layered system, where each layer can only use services provided by the layer immediately below it. Any source code component that does not observe this constraint represents an architecture violation. If not corrected, such violations can transform the architecture into a monolithic block, with adverse effects on understandability, maintainability, and evolvability.

Various approaches have been proposed to address erosion. "These approaches, which include tools, techniques, and processes, are primarily classified into three general categories that attempt to minimize, prevent and repair architecture erosion. Within these broad categories, each approach is further broken down reflecting the high-level strategies adopted to tackle erosion. These are process-oriented architecture conformance, architecture evolution management, architecture design enforcement, architecture to implementation linkage, self-adaptation and architecture restoration techniques consisting of recovery, discovery, and reconciliation."

There are two major techniques to detect architectural violations: reflexion models and domain-specific languages. Reflexion model (RM) techniques compare a high-level model provided by the system's architects with the source code implementation. There are also domain-specific languages with a focus on specifying and checking architectural constraints.

Software Architecture Recovery

Software architecture recovery (or reconstruction, or reverse engineering) includes the methods, techniques, and processes to uncover a software system's architecture from available information, including its implementation and documentation. Architecture recovery is often necessary to make informed decisions in the face of obsolete or out-of-date documentation and architecture erosion: implementation and maintenance decisions diverging from the envisioned architecture. Practices exist to recover software architecture as Static program analysis. This is a part of subjects covered by the Software intelligence practice.

Types of Software Architect

- System architect.
  - Affects one system and builds connections within it.
  - Focuses on the technical component of the development.
  - Helps the project manager to make management decisions.

- ○ Has deep knowledge of the technologies.
- Solution architect.
  - ○ Participates in discussions of business.
  - ○ Creates connections between several systems.
  - ○ Provides communication between several teams.
  - ○ Designs connections between systems.
  - ○ Codes independently only solution prototypes.
  - ○ Acts as a universal soldier of business and technology.
- Enterprise architect.
  - ○ Affects all development of the company.
  - ○ Works with high-level abstractions of the created systems.
  - ○ Provides technical communications throughout the company.
  - ○ Does not interact with the code.
  - ○ Focuses on the business component.
  - ○ Has a broad technical horizon.
  - ○ Owns several domains.

Domain Architects

If the project consists of one or more platforms, each of them requires an expert who will act as a domain architect and perform the following duties:

- Identifying the stakeholders on the project. It is important to note that a domain architect should select stakeholders that affect his platform and work with them.

- Identifying business requirements and requirements of the stakeholders on the project. If the architect finds platform-specific stakeholders, then he/she should find the requirements with the restrictions, specifically for the domain.

- Designing the entire system based on the received requirements. For a domain architect, it is more important not to design an entire system, but to integrate the platform into the project outline. And also, to consider the connections between the components that affect the platform.

- Choosing the technologies for the implementation of each component and connections between the components. Unlike higher-level architects, a domain architect, as a rule, has the greatest impact on the choice of application technologies for her/his platform. For example, in mobile applications the architect deals with such issues as: what kinds of testing to use on the project, whether it needs code generation, how to organize the service and presentation layers, what architectural patterns to use and why it is generally necessary for the project.

- Writing project documentation and its support. If there is an architecture, then it should be documented. Even in terms of one platform. If the architecture is not documented, then it is not architecture. In the mobile development, it can be a scheme for working with databases, a description of network interactions, class diagrams and so on.

- Creating unified development standards in the company. This point is especially suitable for a domain architect, because all standards are usually developed for a specific platform.

- Controlling the architecture during the next iteration of the system release.

A domain architect must control the entire product development cycle. And being the closest person to the technical component of the platform and, at the same time, seeing it as a whole picture, the architect is fully responsible for the quality of the product on a particular platform.

As a result, there is a large number of different types of domain architects:

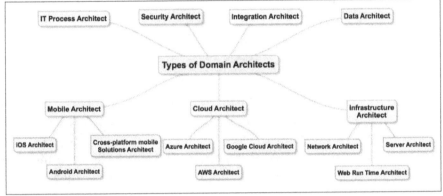

Some types of domain architects

The picture shows only a small part of them. In reality, there are much more of them, as well as various technology stacks.

On the other hand, it is necessary to add the position of the architect only when the corresponding responsibilities are apparent. If you have a project from one platform and two developers, adding an architect's position is redundant and one of the developers can perform this duties.

Why does Software Architect need Certificates

- Customer's requirement. The customer can require certified employees only. This is one of the key points, why you might need certification. For non-technical persons, certificates are one of the few ways to understand that an expert has the skills to perform a particular job.

- If you work on the global market. If you have not been heard about in the country of relocation, even if you are a good and well-known specialist on your market, the certificates will allow you to prove your skills.

- If you want to change your job. The more tags in the resume, the easier it is to change job. But developers know that the more experience they have, the more often the work is looking for them, and not vice versa. For an architect, as for an extremely unique resource on the human resources market, this phrase is even more reasonable.

It is your own decision whether you need a certificate with confirmation of your skills or not. Usually this situational decision is based on current needs.

How to Become Software Architect

Software architects are information technology professionals who design software systems. Some specialize in systems software, while others specialize in applications software. These professionals translate user needs into technical information to create software to meet those needs. Software architects can earn high wages, depending on the types of systems, tools, programming languages and network architecture they're familiar with.

Software Architect Job Information

Job Description

Software architects apply their knowledge of computer science, engineering, and mathematics to design and develop computer programs and applications. They may create new software or modify existing software with the goal of producing an efficient, reliable, and easy-to-maintain product. This profession is extremely client-focused and software architects often communicate with clients throughout the development process to ensure the end product meets expectations.

Duties

Along with assessing clients' needs, software architects establish customized development processes according to the project. This includes determining cost, time, and practicability of the project. They collaborate with and may supervise other IT professionals, such as system analysts, technicians, and computer programmers. Software architects also test and modify software to fix any malfunctions.

Software Architect Requirements and Qualifications

Education Requirements

While some advanced positions may require graduate degrees, most software architects hold bachelor's degrees. Aspiring software architects often major in software engineering, computer science, math, or information systems. A Bachelor of Science in Software Engineering program typically prepares students for positions in software architecture. Curricula typically focus on technical training, computer science theory, and computer systems development. Courses may include:

- Data structures

- Algorithms

- Software engineering

- Quality testing
- Programming languages
- Computer science
- Software architecture

The Role of a Software Architect

1. A software architect needs to interact with clients, product managers, and developers in order to envision, model and provide initial models and designs that can be built. This role also may cover the meeting potential or current customers.

2. A software architect has to constantly review the code to ensure the quality of the design by avoiding complexity, advocating clarity and to do this with the team. This usually requires hands-on work in terms of developing prototypes, contributing code or evaluating technologies.

3. The role of a software architect includes collaborative working with a degree of humility and providing mentoring as required. Such collaboration also allows the architect to become familiar with the skills and interests in the team and to share their knowledge with the rest of the team. Humility is required to ensure that all the team is listened to, as they may have more specific experience or knowledge for the problem at hand.

Taking into account all of the main aspects the software architect role includes, its obvious that this person should have knowledge in programming, management, psychology, communication and even finance. So, what are the main skills and qualities this specialist must have?

The Main Characteristics of a Software Architect

- *Broad and deep technical knowledge.* This should be obvious since one cannot become a software architect with a musical background. The architect usually has knowledge in several technological stacks at a decent level and should have a good understanding of a few other ones. The software architect should also be prepared to compose a large number of technical documentation, reports, and diagrams.

- *Responsibility.* A software architect should understand those architect decisions are usually the most expensive. A person in this position should take the most responsible approach to his work and to the decisions made. If the developer's error costs a couple days of work of one person, then the architect's mistake can cost person-years on complex projects.

- *Communicability.* A good specialist should be able to talk with customers in the language of business, managers of all levels, business analysts and developers in their languages. To explain all the action correctly, a software architect has to grow a natural charisma and ability to convince people. Usually, architects are laconic, eloquent and competent speakers. While software architects participate in discussions they should be able to persuade the others.

- *Management skills.* This includes both organizational and leadership skills. The ability to lead a team, which may be distributed and composed of very different specialists.

- *Stress resistance.* A software architect works with different people from different areas, rapidly changing demands or even with changing business environments. Therefore, it is necessary to be ready for stress and to look for some ways to escape negative emotions. Work is always more pleasant when you're happy.

- *Analytic skills.* One of the most important tasks is the ability to represent an abstract problem in the form of some finite real object of the system, which can be evaluated, designed and developed.

Main Responsibilities of a Software Architect

The most important responsibility is *complete technical support* of the project from the moment of inception, through product release, to development of enhancements. The other responsibilities considered among the main ones are:

- Identifying business requirements and requirements of the stakeholders on the project

- Designing the entire system based on the received requirements

- Choosing the system architecture and each individual component of this system at a high level

- Choosing the technologies for the implementation of each component and connections between the components

- Architectural review

- Code-review

- Writing project documentation and its support

- Creating unified development standards in the company

- Controlling the architecture during the next iteration of the system release

There are a lot. Crafting the right architecture to solve the problem at hand is only part of architects' responsibilities. They must also:

- Control over correct using the architecture

- Control over timing and deadline

- Control over synchronization of the software with the system architecture

- Do performance quality control

- Give input as needed to issues like the tool and environment selection

- Interact with management and stakeholders

- Resolve disputes and make tradeoffs

- Resolve technical problems

- Understand and plan for evolutionary paths

- Plan for new technology insertion
- Manage risk identification and risk mitigation strategies associated with the architecture.

So, to become a software architect, you need to pass a long way of learning and improvement. Understanding several technological stacks is a must: server languages, iOS, Android and more. You have to read a lot of professional literature and find some mentor to ask questions. Don't underestimate the influence of different courses and workshops. Be aware that the path of becoming a software architect will take at least several years.

How to Copyright Software

Copyright protects the original expression of ideas in tangible forms such as literature, music, drama and art. Copyright protection also extends to computer software. A work is automatically subject to copyright as soon as it is recorded in a tangible form.

This means that you do not need to register anywhere to get a copyright - you ALREADY have copyright on any original work that you have created.

The purpose of registering a copyright work is therefore to create an independently verifiable record of the date and content of your work to ensure you can prove your claim in a dispute. Within the US, this is done through the US Copyright Office (and this page explains how to do that). Outside the US, there are many organizations that offer similar services that tend to be a lot faster.

If you are a US citizen there is however a requirement to register with the US Copyright Office before you can take action in a US court.

If you are not a US citizen, find out about copyrights on the World Intellectual Property Organization, (www.wipo.int) as computer programs are NOT on the list of the Berne Convention, but is included in the notion of a production in the literary, scientific and artistic domain.

Steps

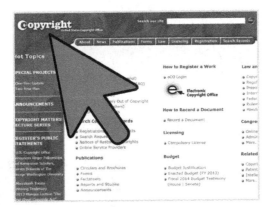

1. Determine how much of what you send to the Copyright Office will be code and how much will be screenshots. As part of the processing for copyrighting software, you will have to send a hard copy

deposit of your software to the Copyright Office. The Copyright Office regards your source or object code and screen displays to be part of the same computer program and thus requires only a single registration to copyright all components of the same software application. However, the Copyright Office presently has no designation for "computer software" as a type of work to be registered on its forms. You have to decide how you plan to register the work under the categories it does have.

- If your software is predominantly text-based, register it as a "literary work."

- If your software uses a lot of pictures or graphics in its display, register it as a "visual arts work."

- If your software uses a lot audio-visual components, such as .avi files, animated graphics or streaming video, register it as a "motion picture/audiovisual work." (Most video games will fall into this category.)

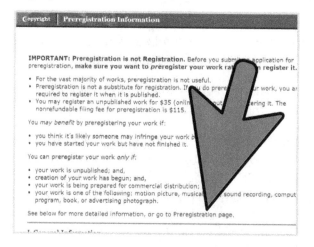

2. Consider pre-registering your software. Preregistration is designed to protect a work still in development from infringement. It does not replace registration, but it allows the developer to sue someone else for infringement that occurs before the final version is released or published. Along with computer software, preregistration is available for motion pictures, compositions of music, sound recordings, photos used in advertising or marketing and literary works to be published in a book.

- Preregistration is available only online. You submit a description of up to 2,000 characters (330 words) of the software, along with a filing fee, payable by credit card, through the Automated Clearing House (ACH) network or from an account previously established with the Copyright Office. (You do not include an actual copy of the code or program screens.)

- Once the Copyright Office processes your preregistration, they'll send you a notification by e-mail with the information you sent, a preregistration number and the date your preregistration was processed and became effective. You can obtain a certified copy of the notification from the Copyright Office's Certifications and Documents section.

- Once you pre-register your work, you must register it within 3 months after you publish or produce it or within a month after you become aware someone has infringed your copyright. If you don't register within this time, any court must dismiss a suit brought prior to or within the first 2 months after publication.

3. File your registration with the Copyright Office. The Copyright Office now permits you to file your registration in 1 of 3 ways: online through its electronic Copyright Office (eCO), completing fill-in Form CO on your personal computer, or obtaining a paper form from the Copyright Office. All 3 methods require you to include payment with your application and permit you to register a single work, multiple published works by the same author or multiple published works collected together for the first time in the same publication on the same date owned by the same person filing the registration.

- To access the electronic filing option, go to the Copyright Office website at http://www.copyright.gov/ and select "electronic Copyright Office." You'll be asked whether you intend to submit an electronic or a hard copy of your work. (You may submit either an electronic or hard copy of any unpublished work with this option.) Using this option lets you file for less money than the other 2 options and also provides you with faster processing, the ability to pay electronically, e-mail acknowledgment of your submission and online tracking of the status of your application.

- Fill-in Form CO can be obtained by selecting "Forms" on the Copyright Office website at http://www.copyright.gov/. This form includes a barcode that permits the Copyright Office to process the form with its scanners; because each barcode is unique to the registration application, you can only use Form CO to register the work for which you requested it. After completing the form on your computer, you then print it out.

- Requests for paper forms must be addressed to the Library of Congress, U.S. Copyright Office-TX, 101 Independence Avenue SE, Washington, DC 20559-6222. Use the same address to submit a copyright registration and your payment by mail; a completed Fill-in Form CO is sent to the same address. (You may also print out your electronic registration form and send it by mail if you wish, but you then pay the higher fee for non-electronic processing.)

- For whichever method you use, fill in the "Year of Completion" with the year you completed work on the computer program and the exact date the version you're seeking to register was first published. Fill in the "Author Created" space with the elements of the software package you're seeking to register, such as just the program itself or the program and its accompanying documentation. Fill in the "Limitation of Claim" if you created the program using a lot of previously published code and subroutines or an authoring tool; use the "Material excluded" section to list those subroutines (or simply state "Previous version") and the "New material included" section to list the parts you're actually claiming copyright for, such as new code or editing of existing code.

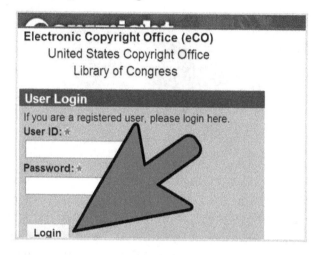

4. Deposit a copy of your work with the Copyright Office. If your software is unpublished, you may submit the copy either electronically in PDF format or as a printed copy, depending on whether you're submitting the accompanying application electronically or by hard copy. If you're submitting a published copy of your software, you must submit a hard copy regardless of which filing method you use.

- If your program does not contain any trade secrets, you need to submit a paper or microform hard copy of the first and last 25 pages of source code, or the entire source code if it runs less than 50 pages. (If the program is written in a scripted language such as Hyper-Card, the script is treated as source code.) You may substitute object code for the source code, providing you accompany it with a written statement that the object code contains copyrightable authorship.

- If your program does contain trade secrets, you may submit the first and last 25 pages of source code or all the source code if it runs less than 50 pages, with the source code containing your trade secrets blocked out. You can also send just the first and last 10 pages of source code, if none of those pages contain trade secrets, or any 10 consecutive pages of source code without trade secrets and the first and last 25 pages of object code. This must be accompanied by a letter stating that the code contains trade secrets.

- If the program is structured in such a way that there's no definable beginning or end to the source code, you can decide which sections of the code represent the first and last pages.

- If the source code has revisions, and the revisions are not included in any of the portions of code described above, you need to include 20 consecutive pages of code with the revisions and no trade secrets or any 50 pages of code that include the revisions and have any trade secrets blocked out.

- You have the option as to whether or not to include screenshots as part of your deposit if you filled in the "Author Created" section of your copyright registration form as "Author

Created." If, instead, you filled it in as "Computer program, including text and screen displays" or similar, then you must include screenshots for all the screens you wish to register. (If the screens are displayed in a user manual, sending the manual is an acceptable way to send in the screenshots.) If you're registering audiovisual displays, you can do so on 1/2-inch VHS tape, CD-ROM or DVD-ROM, or upload the file if it is small enough.

- If your software has been published on CD-ROM or DVD-ROM, you must include a copy of the disc, with any accompanying operating software and user manual. (If the manual is in printed form, you must include a hard copy of the manual; a PDF copy is not acceptable as a substitute.)

How to Patent Software

An invention implemented in software may be patentable in the United States, provided it is unique and tied to a machine or transformation. Strictly speaking, you aren't patenting the software itself. Rather, you're patenting one or more inventions embodied within the software. Only with copyright can you protect the code of the software itself. You begin the process by applying for a patent with the U.S. Patent and Trademark Office (USPTO).

Part 1. Determining Eligibility

1. Categorize your invention. Typically a software-based invention is categorized as a process, which is one of the four categories of subject matter invention that are eligible for patent protection.

- As you look at how your software will be used – for example, whether it will be incorporated directly into a computer or distributed separately from the hardware that runs it – you'll gain an understanding of what unique parts of your software must be protected from competitors.

- These processes are typically the inventions that need patent protection. In most cases they solve a problem. For example, suppose you create software that when installed in a washing machine turns the machine off if it is about to overflow. Your patent will protect your process of detecting an imminent overflow and shutting down the machine.

2. Define the invention. To be patentable, you must have an invention within your software that is new and non-obvious.

- Additionally, your invention must be tied to a machine or transformation of materials. This essentially means that the invented process requires a machine to complete essential steps. To return to the washing machine example, your invention clearly is tied to the machine because your software causes the on-board computer of a washing machine to accomplish something directly.

- Your claims cannot be based on abstract ideas or concepts to be eligible for patent protection. In other words, you can't patent a mathematical formula, but you might be able to patent a machine that implements a particular application of that formula.

- For example, suppose you've found an equation enabling a computer to navigate a space craft to specific coordinates in space. You would not be able to patent the equation, but you could patent the implementation in software that you designed to be installed in, let's say, the space shuttle.

3. Research the prior art. Before you file for your patent, you must complete a search of "the prior art". Technically, this includes searching worldwide for patents, applications for patents, any publications disclosing inventions, and any public use of an identical or similar invention.

- The goal is to determine whether your invention contributes to the "state of the art" in a way that justifies granting you a patent.

- If you've never performed a search for prior art, the USPTO recommends hiring a registered attorney or agent to help you conduct your search. If you have limited resources, you may be able to find an attorney to work for you for free or at a drastically reduced cost.

- If you want to conduct the patent portion of the search yourself, you may do so using the USPTO's Patent Full Text Database, which contains all patent applications and granted patents from 1976 to the present.

- Your patent search will also enable you to determine that your invention has never been declared to be "obvious." To be patentable, your invention must be "non-obvious" from the viewpoint of someone who is skilled in the field and has access to the existing knowledge about inventions in that field, whether implemented in hardware or software.

- Once you find relevant patents or patent applications, you can use their lists of cited references to delve more deeply into other related publications or uses, all of which form part of the prior art in the field.

- The most relevant references you find will be important to the structure of your patent application -- specifically: your "claims" -- and references must be submitted with your application, so keep track of what you find.

- Another fringe benefit of a comprehensive patent search is the early identification of existing patents of others for which you may need a license prior to selling your own implementation.

Part 2. Filing A Provisional Application

1. Use a provisional application to buy yourself time. A non-provisional application takes a lot of time to complete and process, but a provisional application gives you the benefit of proving invention priority at an earlier effective date.

- Provisional applications are relatively inexpensive and do not require many of the complications of the longer, non-provisional applications.

- Your provisional application allows you to use the words "patent pending" in relation to your invention for up to 12 months while you work on your non-provisional application.

However, it may be beneficial to keep your invention confidential for as long as possible, under highly competitive circumstances. For example, if it takes five years to get your patent issued, your competitors may have already saturated the market with their knock-offs, undermining the value of your patent.

- You may file a provisional or non-provisional application in the USA any time within 12 months of the first public disclosure or sale of your invention.

- However, most other countries have no such "grace period" for filing your application. You generally must file prior to any public use or disclosure of your invention, if you plan to obtain a patent outside the USA. In other words, your own premature disclosure or sale will become prior art that defeats your own patents nearly everywhere outside of the USA. A provisional application may be an inexpensive and quick means to satisfy that filing obligation.

- You are allowed to file additional provisional applications at any time, as you find new features not previously disclosed, and for which you may later want to claim the earliest possible priority.

2. Complete your provisional application. It must include a complete written description of the invention along with the names of all inventors.

- To be complete, your provisional application must be accompanied by the filing fee and a cover sheet that identifies the application as a provisional patent application and lists the names and addresses of all inventors, the title of the invention, the name and registration number of any attorneys or agents who worked with you to prepare your application, and the address you intend to use for correspondence with the USPTO.

- You are strongly urged to include any drawings necessary for someone to understand your invention, such as software flow charts and diagrams of any special computer interface you invented.

- You should be as specific as you can about your invention, as you currently understand it. You should later review your provisional applications to make sure you haven't omitted anything, so you can file further versions along the way, as necessary.

3. File your provisional application. Once you've completed your provisional application, you can file it using the USPTO's electronic filing system.

- If you prefer to use the mail, you can send a hard copy of your application along with the filing fee to: Commissioner for Patents, P.O. Box 1450, Alexandria, VA 22313-1450.

- In either case, you will get a serial number and filing date for your application. You have up to one year from that filing date in which to claim priority of your provisional application within a non-provisional application.

- Your provisional application is not examined for patentability and will not be published. If you fail to submit a complete cover sheet and fees, or to later claim its priority within a year, its file will become abandoned and disposed of.

Part 3. Filing A Non-Provisional Application

1. Assess the commercial viability of your software. Because applying for patents is much more expensive and time-consuming than registering copyrights, you should make a realistic projection of how much money you expect to make with your software before you jump into the patent application process.

- Financial considerations include coming up with projections for not only the retail value of copies you expect to distribute, but also potential license fees, the wholesale value of your invention, tempered with the costs to operate a manufacturing, distribution and support structure yourself, not to mention the potentially huge expense of attempting to enforce even a single patent in the USA.

2.Consider hiring a registered attorney or agent. Non-provisional patent applications are extremely complex, and patent examiners expect the application to be written and compiled in a specific way. The USPTO recommends you hire someone with experience to help you draw up your non-provisional application, so you don't waste time and money on an incomplete or incorrect application.

3. Draft your non-provisional application. Your application will include a number of required forms. While you may find forms elsewhere, the USPTO recommends you use the forms it provides to make sure everything is correct.

- The application transmittal and fee transmittal forms provide a list of the elements of your application and the fees being submitted. You must sign each of these forms after filling them out and include them with your application.

- The application data sheet is similar to the cover sheet included with the provisional application and must be filed to claim the benefit of the prior-filed provisional application.

- Your specification includes documents that describe your invention in full, clear, and exact terms, including how your invention is made and/or used. A software patent application approaches the software's use from an end-user's perspective. It also discusses its use and structure from a systems point of view and the computer's point of view.

- The specification includes a number of documents, such as the background and summary of your invention, a detailed description including drawings, and a list of the claims you are making with respect to your invention.

- Your application will close with the inventor's oath or declaration, in which you declare that you made the application and that you are the original inventor of the invention claimed in the application. If you make an oath, it must be signed in the presence of a notary public. A declaration does not require a notary or any other witness but must be signed.

4. Prepare to file electronically. Before you file your non-provisional application, you must determine how much the processing fees will be for your application and apply for a customer number and digital certificate.

- Your processing fees will depend on the number of claims you have. The total amount is reduced if you qualify as a small entity or a micro entity. Small entities generally are individuals or small businesses with fewer than 500 employees. Micro entities are small entities with fewer than four non-provisional utility patents and income less than three times the median household income. For example, in 2014, the applicant would have to have earned less than $155,817 to qualify as a micro entity.

- If you claim small or micro entity status, you must fill out an additional form certifying that status and include it with your application and supplemental statements with any subsequent filing fees. If your fee status changes at any time, you must file the appropriate fees for your new status, as of the next required filing.

5. File your application using the electronic filing system. Once you've completed all the forms in the packet, you can submit them along with your filing fee using the USPTO's filing system.

6. Wait for a response from the USPTO. It provides a calculator on its website that you can use to estimate how long it will take to receive the first office action on your patent.

- If you don't hear anything within a year or so, it is your obligation to investigate where things are before your file accidentally becomes "abandoned".

- Similarly, don't lose track of your deadlines on any international patent applications you may want to file.

7. File replies, appeals, or requests for reconsideration as necessary. Your patent examiner will review your patent application and any claims you make. You may argue the patentability of those claims, but you cannot alter your patent application once it's filed.

- You may, however, amend your claims, to the extent necessary to "narrow" them, but may not add any "new matter" to your application, i.e., something not already disclosed in your original applications (provisional and non-provisional, or otherwise "pending" in this application file).

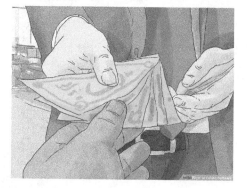

8. Pay the issue fee and publication fee. If the patent examiner raises any objections and you are able to overcome them, you'll be sent a "notice of allowance" and given a fee statement. You will

then have your patent issued as soon as you pay the required issuance fees and comply with any other requirements stated in the notice.

- It may be worth noting that the issuance date terminates the "pendency" of your patent application, so you may want to file other applications for related inventions prior to having your first one issued. That way, they may claim the earliest priority date from your first patent that remains "co-pending". Your patent attorney can explain the intricacies of "continuation-in-part", "divisionals" and related tactics.

9. Maintain your patent. To keep patent protection, you must pay maintenance fees 3.5, 7.5, and 11.5 years after your patent is granted.

- As with other USPTO fees, you will pay lower maintenance fees if you qualify as a small entity or a micro entity.

- USPTO fees change occasionally, so you'll need to check the fee schedule to find out how much you owe. Recently the fees for a small entity were $800 after 3.5 years, $1,800 after 7.5 years, and $3,700 after 11.5 years.

Part 4. Considering Copyright Protection

1. Understand the difference between a patent and a copyright. Copyright protects the particular expression of your process, while a patent protects the process itself.

- Copyright is simpler, in that it automatically begins from the moment your software is created and lasts many years after your death. A patent, on the other hand, requires an acceptable invention disclosure and lasts only around 20 years.

- Copyright registration is easy, inexpensive, and can be completed on your own, while a full patent application typically requires legal assistance.

- Some countries do not recognize patents of software-related inventions. This can be a problem if you plan to sell your program globally.

- Keep in mind that the law does not technically require any code to be written for the software in order for it to be patentable, however, any original code that is written would be covered by your copyright.

- If you have written basic code for the software, a registered copyright can provide a layer of protection for your disclosure while you complete the patent application process, if you decide to do so. Copyright refers only to the form of the work of authorship, not to any functions or systems it may describe. If someone obtains your software and rewrites it to duplicate the functions, it would not be a copyright infringement.

- Also keep in mind that when you register a claim to a copyright, you are making a public record, so if you do plan on filing a patent application you should consider the patent disclosure grace periods described above. You may be allowed to deposit only small portions of your software, with redacted trade secrets, in some circumstances.

2. Fill out a copyright registration form. You may register your copyright either by using the eCO electronic system or by filling out a paper form and mailing it to the Copyright Office along with a check for your fees and copies of your software.

- The Copyright Office recommends using the electronic system, which is faster and allows you to monitor the status of your registration online.

- If you are registering with a paper form, you should either fill it in on your computer or write in your information by hand using a black pen.

3. File your copyright registration. When you file for copyright you must send your application, the filing fee, and one copy of your software for deposit with the Library of Congress.

- The filing fee is $35 if you use the online system and $85 if you mail a paper application.

- If your work has been published, and you are filing a hard copy, you may be required to file two copies of the best edition of your work.

- Paper applications should be accompanied by your deposit (copy) materials and a nonrefundable filing fee in the form of a check or money order payable to the Register of Copyrights. Mail these items to the Library of Congress, Copyright Office-TX, 101 Independence Avenue SE, Washington, DC 20559. Your online application may be completed using a credit card, debit card, ACH debit, or by reference to a "deposit account" you have set up in the Copyright Office.

- If there are any problems found during the examination of your claim of copyright, you will be notified and given time to correct any errors.

Careers in Software Development

Software development encompasses the development of a wide range of software operating systems, business applications, games, computer applications and network control systems. This allows specializations in a number of fields. Some of the professionals working in this domain are software analysts, software managers, software developers and programmers, consultants, software engineers, etc. This chapter has been carefully written to provide an overview of such software development careers and the ways to become successful professionals in these domains.

How to get a Software Development Job

Software developers are in high demand currently and that demand is projected to increase in the near future. If you enjoy working with computers, math, and have a good understanding of what users of software need you might find work as a software developer enjoyable. There are many ways to get started finding work as a software developer and learning some of them can help make your job search a success.

Part 1. Obtaining Necessary Education and Skills

1. Discover more about the position. Before you pursue a career in software development it can helpful to learn the details about the position. Knowing more about your future as a software developer will help you to better plan your path to obtaining the position and help you determine if it's a good fit for you.

- On average software developers earn around $90,000 annually.

- There is a large demand for software developers and the position is expected to grow up to 22% by 2022.

- Software developers build computer programs that either run applications or build the applications themselves.

2. Select a technical focus. Although having a well rounded skill set and education will help you to obtain a position as a software engineer, choosing some specific skills to focus on can be a good idea. By building strong skills in a few areas you will be able to find a position that best suits your own career interests in software development.

- Think about what kinds of software you want to develop and learn skills applicable to them.

- For example, you may want to focus on game development, app development, website development, or software development.

- Pick a programming language that you enjoy and want to learn more about.

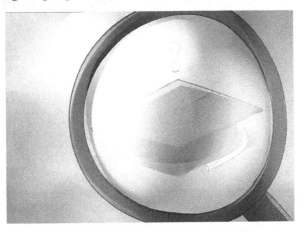

3. Find a school. Although it is possible to be self-taught and still find employment as a software developer, attending classes can be a good way to obtain the skills and education required for the position. Search for a college, university, or other course that has a program suited to your interests in the field of software development.

- Most software developers begin working after obtaining their bachelors degree.

- Both computer science and software engineering can be good choices when selecting a major.

- Although demonstrable skills can be enough to get a job, having an education in addition to those skills will help.

4. Supplement your education and skills. Branching out from your main areas of study can be a good way to broaden your understanding of the field and gain additional skills. Being well rounded and informed will make you more appealing to potential employers.

- Study topics that you find interesting that lie outside your course material.

- Don't stop learning. Technology develops and changes quickly and your knowledge and skills will have to reflect this.

- Expanding your skill set will make you more appealing to employers.

5. Get as much experience as possible. Beyond learning the ideas and concepts behind being a software developer you will want to get as much hands-on practice as you can. By actually implementing what you have been learning you will continue the learning process and build some examples that you can share with potential employers.

- Building and developing your own projects will let you practice your skills.

- Having software that you have developed can be a great addition to your resume.

- Work on open source projects or offer some projects for free to build a portfolio.

Part 2. Preparing Your Resume

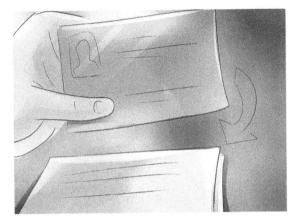

1. Include your contact information. The point of your resume will be to allow your potential employer to evaluate your skills and contact you for an interview. All parts of the resume are important but without your contact information you will not be able to be contacted even if your skills are outstanding. Include the following information about yourself at the top of your resume:

- Your full name.

- Your address.

- Phone numbers.

- An email address.

- Personal websites that highlight your previous and relevant work.

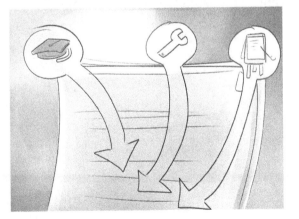

2. Prepare a detailed list of your education, training, and skills. Part of any good resume is to outline your skills and education. This should be a clear and detailed list of your qualifications for the position which will demonstrate the assets you are offering to bring to the employer if hired. Include the following information regarding your education: •The full name of any institutions you attended.

- Include the address of those institutions.

- When you graduated and what degree you earned.

- Additional minors or majors.

- Including your GPA can demonstrate your academic achievements.

3. Make a section to show your past employment. Listing your past employers is a requirement for most resumes. In listing who you worked for last you demonstrate what you have already accomplished professionally and what duties you performed in those roles. Review the following details that you should include for your past employers:

- Full name of the employer

- The date you were hired and the date you left.

- Where that employer was located.

- Focus on your roles and responsibilities with that employer.

4. Consider including hobbies. After you have detailed your professional skills and qualifications you can also include relevant hobbies. These hobbies should demonstrate your skill and passion for software development even further. Only include your hobbies if you have enough space to do so as this section is optional on your resume.

- Only include hobbies relevant to the position you are applying for.

- For example, you might program and develop games for the Android platform as a hobby.

- Another example would be any community events you organized that might demonstrate leadership.

- Include your hobbies only if you have room on your resume to do so.

5. Keep your resume the right length. Employers are likely to receive a large amount of resumes that they will need to read through quickly. If your resume is too long or short this can automatically cause you to be rejected for the position. Strive to keep your resume at the appropriate length for the position you are applying for.

- Many employers require your resume to be only one page in length.

- If you are seeking work fresh out of college then a one page resume is likely acceptable.

- Longer resumes will be required only if you have the relevant work experience to match.

Part 3. Searching For A Position

1. Look locally. If you don't plan on relocation you can check locally for any software development jobs that might have become available. These positions might be found in local publications such as newspapers or on-line by searching for jobs in your area.

- Local publications will often have sections for employers to list open positions.

- If there is a company or employer nearby you might try inquiring directly or leaving your resume with them.

2. Search for openings with specific companies. You may have a specific company in mind that you have always wanted to work for. If this is the case you will want to inquire directly with that company to see if they have an software development positions currently open. Check on-line or contact via email or phone to learn if your desired company is hiring.

- Many companies offer information about available positions directly on their website.

- Always follow the instructions that the company lists when submitting your resume or application.

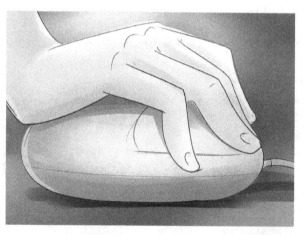

3. Browse major job and career websites. There are many large sites that employers and employees can make use of to find work or to offer it. Signing up for these sites will allow you to easily submit your resume and apply to any open software development positions that you might find.

- Websites like http://www.indeed.com/ or http://www.monster.com/ are good places to post your resume and search for software development positions.

- Certain sites such as https://www.linkedin.com/ allow you to create professional profile, resume and let you network with other professionals to look for software development opportunities.

Part 4. Interviewing Well

1. Think of questions to ask. Although you will likely be the one answering most of the questions during your interview it is good practice to come prepared with questions of your own. Asking questions can show your interest, attention to detail, and seriousness in regards to the interview and the position you are seeking.

- Try to have at least two or three thoughtful questions to ask.

- If a question was answered during the course of the interview you can state this to demonstrate that you had prepared the question.

- An example would be to ask about the companies unique strengths or how they would describe an ideal employee.

- Don't ask about salary.

2. Research the employer. Don't forget that the interview process goes two ways. While you are being evaluated by the employer you should also be evaluating the company. Doing some research about the company will help you appear knowledgeable, interested and informed during the interview as well as let you decide if the employer is one you want to work for.

- Spend some time looking into the history of the company.

- Inquire about the companies potential and future plans.

- Read up on company policy and mission statements.

3. Practice your interview. Interviews can be high-stress situations. Practicing the interview before you enter into it can help you feel confident and remove some of the stress that can come with the process. Practice what you want to say during your interview, how you want to present yourself, and key concepts you want to focus on in order to do your best and relax when interviewing.

- Mock-interview services are often available. These will test, evaluate, and allow you to improve you interviewing skills.

- You can try practicing with a friend or family remember.

- Forming and practicing what you want to say can make it easier to repeat during the interview.

- Think about the key aspects of your skills and personality that you want to convey.

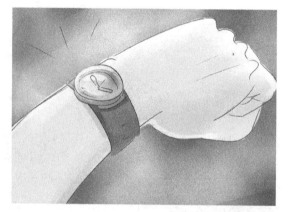

4. Arrive early. Part of interviewing well is arriving to it early. The time you arrive will demonstrate your punctuality and your ability to follow a schedule. Always plan your trip to the interview and make sure you allow yourself enough time to arrive early.

- Arriving late will likely cause you to no longer be considered for the position.

- Arriving too early can send the wrong message and may hurt your chances.

- Arriving about five to ten minutes early will allow you time to collect your thoughts and will make a good impression.

- Planning your route out ahead will help you arrive right when you intend to.

Software Analysts

In a software development team, a software analyst is the person who studies the software application domain, prepares software requirements, and specification (Software Requirements Specification) documents. The software analyst is the seam between the software users and the software developers. They convey the demands of software users to the developers.

A software analyst is expected to have the following skills:

- Working knowledge of software technology
- Computer programming experience and expertise
- General business knowledge
- Problem solving and problem reduction skills
- Interpersonal relation skills
- Flexibility and adaptability

How to Become Software Analyst

There are four steps required to become a software analyst: post-secondary education, computer software work experience, apply for a job as a software analyst, and complete the job interview process. A computer software analyst is responsible for reviewing specifications, testing programs, working with programmers and developers, and writing documentation. As a software analyst, it is important to understand your role in the software development process. The programmers and developers create the software code or programming to meet their understanding of the user requirements. It is the responsibility of the software analyst to ensure the work product meets those needs, test the product quality, and explain the functionality to the users.

People who are detail oriented, focused and enjoy working with computers find this type of career rewarding. There is a certain level of people interaction, but the majority of the work is independent and can be quite solitary. One of the most common tests to identify a good software analyst is to assign a complex puzzle. People who enjoy a challenge and have a knack for solving the puzzle are naturally inclined to be analysts.

The first requirement to become a software analyst is to obtain a post-secondary education. There is no specific degree or diploma program in software analysis, instead, most candidates complete a degree in computer science, computer programming, or math. It is important to note that the most prestigious companies will ask for a copy of your transcript to review the marks achieved in the senior analysis classes.

Work experience as a software analyst can include volunteer opportunities or internships arranged through your college or university. Another popular method of gaining work experience is to develop your own computer software. A small project will be fine, but the ability to take a project from concept to completion provides valuable insight into the tasks of a programmer and the common issues with functionality, user interfaces, and other items that will need to be reviewed as a software analyst.

Take the time to proofread your resume and cover letter, double checking for any grammar or spelling mistakes when applying to become a software analyst. Attention to detail, focus, and quality output are all part of this job, and a resume with errors indicates sloppiness. Invest the time to research the company and try to tailor your cover letter to address specific items in the job posting.

During the job interview process, to become a software analyst, be prepared for a software analyst test. This test is usually to review a fairly simple program, determine what's working or not working and recommend corrections. The skills being tested include analysis, troubleshooting, use of appropriate terminology, and the application of industry standard quality tests.

Software Management

Software managers are responsible for overseeing and coordinating the people, resources and processes required to deliver new software or upgrade existing products. In smaller companies, software managers may take a hands-on role in software development. However, their primary role is project management, coordinating the work of other software professionals.

Development Strategy

Software managers work closely with business managers or marketing professionals to identify the requirements for new software programs. If they are developing software for internal use, they identify the functional requirements of the departments that will use the programs. To develop software for customers, they identify market requirements and review the performance of existing competitive programs. The functional requirements provide the basis for a product development strategy that gives the software team a clear sense of direction.

Team Management

Managers identify the skills they need for each development project and recruit team members. If the team members don't have the required skills, software managers organize training programs or work with external contractors or consultants who offer those skills. They monitor the performance of team members against strategic targets and provide mentoring or training, if necessary.

Team Resources

Managers ensure that teams have access to the resources they need, such as computing systems, development tools and communications. Resource requirements vary at different stages of software development, so managers monitor progress to ensure that the team does not encounter obstacles. Software developers can utilize cloud computing to scale-up their computing resources in line with project requirements. They may rent additional computing capacity from a service provider, rather than investing in permanent infrastructure.

Scheduling

To ensure that teams complete projects on time, software managers establish schedules. If they are developing software for external customers, they coordinate development schedules with the release dates planned by the marketing team. For new product releases, software managers aim to minimize development time so that they can get the product to market in the shortest possible time.

Project Management

Software managers monitor progress against intermediate and final development targets. They conduct regular team meetings to review progress and to identify potential obstacles to completion. Managers also monitor quality to ensure that products meet their technical and business objectives. In addition to regular development team meetings, software managers also schedule meetings with other stakeholders, such as department managers and marketing professionals to update them on the project and obtain feedback.

How to become a Certified Software Manager

A certified software manager (CSM) helps create and manage various software policies within an organization. He or she particularly deals with the issues of software piracy and licensing requirements and periodically performs audits to make sure the company is following the legal policies required by software vendors. Although a CSM usually works in a technology company, he or she also may work as a legal representative or human resources manager. If you want to become a certified software manager, then you initially need to pass the certification exam. You also should have experience in an information technology position and will need to meet continuing education requirements to keep the certification.

Although there is no professional experience requirement to become a certified software manager, those pursuing the certification typically have experience in a role related to computer software, systems management or asset management. Rather than intending to help you find a job, the certification is geared more toward helping you gain more responsibility in your current organization. It is common for existing system administrators and software analysts to pursue the CSM certification. Those considering careers in law or human resources also may find the exam's study material useful, although earning the CSM credential may not specifically be a job requirement.

There are various seminars and self-study courses available to prepare you to become a certified software manager. Although it is recommended that you attend a course at a training school or on the Internet, you also can purchase the official student manual and study at your own pace. The course and student manual cover copyright laws, penalties for infringement, types of licensing agreements, procedures for software license auditing, and software management plans. If you take an official online or on-campus course, you will gain experience through case studies, practice exam questions and training exercises that will give you better insight on the skills needed on the job.

After you study using the student manual or complete your training course, you should be ready to take the certification exam. If you take a course, you will likely complete the exam on the last day of your training. Those who study for the exam on their own can register for the exam whenever they feel prepared. The exam is given on the Internet, and you can sign up online, via fax or through the mail. After you pass, you are considered a certified software manager, and you'll need to retake the exam every three years to maintain the credential.

Software Developer

Software developers are the creative minds behind computer programs. Some develop the applications that allow people to do specific tasks on a computer or another device. Others develop the underlying systems that run the devices or that control networks.

Duties of Software Developers

Software developers typically do the following:

- Analyze users' needs and then design, test, and develop software to meet those needs

- Recommend software upgrades for customers' existing programs and systems

- Design each piece of an application or system and plan how the pieces will work together

- Create a variety of models and diagrams (such as flowcharts) that show programmers the software code needed for an application

- Ensure that a program continues to function normally through software maintenance and testing

- Document every aspect of an application or system as a reference for future maintenance and upgrades

- Collaborate with other computer specialists to create optimum software.

Software developers are in charge of the entire development process for a software program. They may begin by asking how the customer plans to use the software. They must identify the core functionality that users need from software programs. Software developers must also determine user requirements that are unrelated to the functions of the software, such as the level of security and performance needs. They design the program and then give instructions to programmers, who write computer code and test it.

If the program does not work as expected or if testers find it too difficult to use, software developers go back to the design process to fix the problems or improve the program. After the program is released to the customer, a developer may perform upgrades and maintenance.

Developers usually work closely with computer programmers. However, in some companies, developers write code themselves instead of giving instructions to programmers.

Developers who supervise a software project from the planning stages through implementation sometimes are called information technology (IT) project managers. These workers monitor the project's progress to ensure that it meets deadlines, standards, and cost targets. IT project managers who plan and direct an organization's IT department or IT policies are included in the profile on computer and information systems managers.

The following are examples of types of software developers:

Applications software developers design computer applications, such as word processors and games, for consumers. They may create custom software for a specific customer or commercial software to be sold to the general public. Some applications software developers create complex databases for organizations. They also create programs that people use over the Internet and within a company's intranet.

Systems software developers create the systems that keep computers functioning properly. These could be operating systems for computers that the general public buys or systems built specifically for an organization. Often, systems software developers also build the system's interface, which is what allows users to interact with the computer. Systems software developers create the operating systems that control most of the consumer electronics in use today, including those used by cell phones and cars.

How to become a Software Developer

Software developers usually have a bachelor's degree in computer science and strong computer programming skills.

Education for Software Developers

Software developers usually have a bachelor's degree, typically in computer science, software engineering, or a related field. Computer science degree programs are the most common, because they tend to cover a broad range of topics. Students should focus on classes related to building software to better prepare themselves for work in the occupation. Many students gain experience in software development by completing an internship at a software company while in college. For some positions, employers may prefer that applicants have a master's degree.

Although writing code is not their first priority, developers must have a strong background in computer programming. They usually gain this experience in school. Throughout their career, developers must keep up to date on new tools and computer languages.

Software developers also need skills related to the industry in which they work. Developers working in a bank, for example, should have knowledge of finance so that they can understand a bank's computing needs.

Advancement for Software Developers

Software developers can advance to become information technology (IT) project managers, also called computer and information systems managers, a position in which they oversee the software development process.

Important Qualities for Software Developers

Analytical skills. Developers must analyze users' needs and then design software to meet those needs.

Communication skills. Developers must be able to give clear instructions to others working on a project. They must also explain to their customers how the software works and answer any questions that arise.

Creativity. Developers are the creative minds behind new computer software.

Detail oriented. Developers often work on many parts of an application or system at the same time and must therefore be able to concentrate and pay attention to detail.

Interpersonal skills. Software developers must be able to work well with others who contribute to designing, developing, and programming successful software.

Problem-solving skills. Because developers are in charge of software from beginning to end, they must be able to solve problems that arise throughout the design process.

How to Develop Software

Being a software developer is a lucrative career plan. Those are people with some serious marketable skills. But what exactly are they doing? Since you probably can't beat 'em, you'll have to join 'em. Do you have the tech-savviness and the audience relatability to develop a good product? With a bit of brainstorming - and, of course, starting with Step 1 below - you will.

Part 1. Learning the Ropes

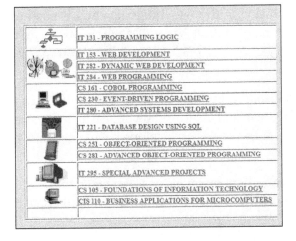

1. Determine which basic type of software development interests you. There are two basic camps of software development: Applications Development and Systems Development. Applications Development is focused on creating programs that meet the users' needs. These can range from mobile phone apps, to high-production video games, to enterprise-level accounting software. Systems Development is focused on creating and maintaining operating systems using life-cycle development. Systems Development often involves network operability and data security.

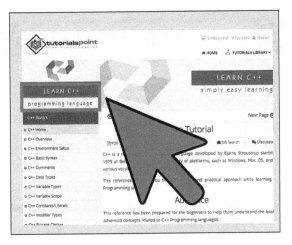

2. Teach yourself a programming language. Anyone can come up with ideas, but a developer will be able to turn those ideas into something tangible. Even if you only want to work on the design aspects of software, you should have some familiarity with coding and be able to create basic prototypes. There are a huge variety of programming languages that you can teach yourself. Some of the more useful and important ones include:

- C - C is one of the older languages still in use, and is the basis for most of the other languages on this list. C is used to develop low-level programs, and works very closely with the computer's hardware.

- C++ - This is the object-oriented version of C, and is the most popular programming language in the world. Programs such as Chrome, Firefox, Photoshop, and many others are all built with C++. It is also a very popular language for creating video games. C++ developers are almost always in very high demand.

- Java - This is an evolution of the C++ language, and is used to due its ease of portability. Almost any system can run a Java Virtual Machine, allowing it to run Java software. It is widely used in video games and business software, and many people recommend it as an essential language.

- C# - C# is a Windows-based language that is part of the .NET framework from Microsoft. It is closely related to Java and C++, and if you learn Java you can quickly transition to C#. This language is especially useful for developers working with Windows or Windows Phone software.

- Objective-C - This is another cousin of the C language that is specifically designed for Apple systems. It sees immense popularity in iPhone and iPad apps. It is a great language to learn as a freelancer.

- Python - This is an incredibly easy language to learn, one of the easiest. Python specializes in web development.

- PHP - This isn't exactly software development, but PHP is essential if you are interested in getting into web development. There is always lots of work for PHP developers, though it isn't as lucrative as software development.

3. Find resources to help you learn. Most bookstores have entire sections dedicated to programming books, and there are tons available on Amazon and other e-tailers. A well-written programming book will likely be the best resource you can have, and will allow you to quickly reference it while working on projects.

- Beyond books, the internet is an endless treasure-trove of guides and tutorials. Search for guides on the language of your choice on sites such as CodeAcademy, Code.org, Bento, Udacity, Udemy, Khan Academy, W3Schools, and many more.

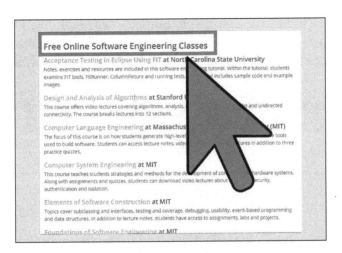

4. Take some classes. While you don't need a full-on degree in order to get into software development, it can't hurt to take a few classes at your local community college or learning center. This will give you the benefit of one-on-one instruction, and you will be challenged to solve problems that you likely wouldn't if you were learning on your own.

- Classes cost money, so make sure that you are signing up for classes that will help you learn what you want to know.

- While many developers are able to enter the industry based purely on the merits of their skills, you'll help yourself stand out from the pack if you have a bachelor's degree in computer science from a four-year university. A degree will give you a wider background of knowledge and will give you access to additional helpful classes such as math and logic.

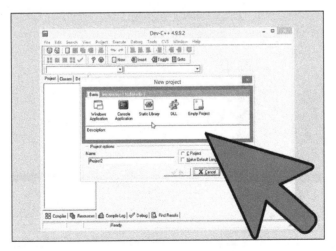

5. Work on pet projects. Before you start trying to apply your new programming skills to real-world jobs, work on some projects for yourself. Challenge yourself to solve problems using your programming language. Not only will this help develop your skills, it will also help build your resume.

- For example, instead of using your computer's calendar program to stay organized, try designing your own.

- If you're interested in video game development, work on simple games that don't focus on graphics or complex mechanics. Instead, focus on making them fun and unique. A collection of small games that you created yourself will look great in your portfolio.

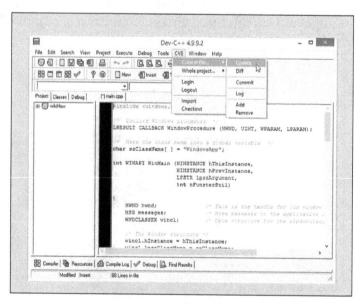

6. Ask questions. The internet is a fantastic way to connect with other developers. If you find yourself stumped on one of your projects, ask for help on sites such as StackOverflow. make sure that you ask in an intelligent manner and can prove that you have already tried several possible solutions.

7. Practice every day. Work on your pet projects every day, even if only for an hour. This will help you stay fresh and constantly learn new techniques. Many developers have had success learning a language by ensuring that they are exposed to it on a daily basis.

- Set a time every day that you can dedicate to coding, or set a deadline that you need to be finished by. Try to work on your projects every day during the week so you can relax on your weekend.

Part 2. Developing a Program

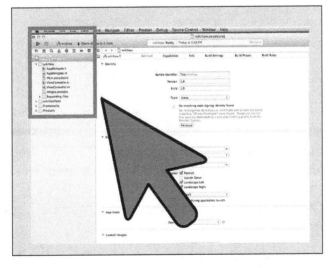

1. Brainstorm ideas. A good program will perform a task that makes life easier for the user. Look at the software that is currently available for the task you want to perform, and see if there are ways that the process could be easier or smoother. A successful program is one that users will find a lot of utility in.

- Examine your daily tasks on your computer. Is there some way that you could automate a portion of those tasks with a program?

- Write down every idea. Even if it seems silly or outlandish at the time, it could change into something useful or even brilliant.

- Examine other programs. What do they do? How could they do it better? What are they missing? Answering these questions can help you come up with ideas for your own take on it.

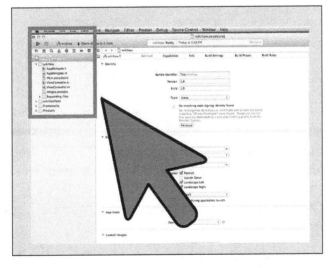

2. Write a design document. This document will outline the features and what you intend to achieve with the project. Referring to the design document during the development process will help keep your project on track and focused. See this guide for details on writing the document.

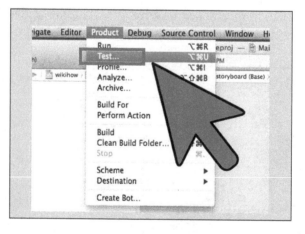

3. Create a prototype. This is a basic program that shows off the functionality that you're aiming to achieve. A prototype is a quick program, and should be iterated on until you find a design that works. For example, if you are creating a calendar program, your prototype would be a basic calendar (with correct dates.) and a way to add events to it.

- Your prototype will change often during the development cycle as you come up with new ways to tackle problems or think of an idea later that you want to incorporate.

- The prototype doesn't have to be pretty. In fact, art and design should be one of the last things you focus on. Using the calendar example again, your prototype should most likely just be text.

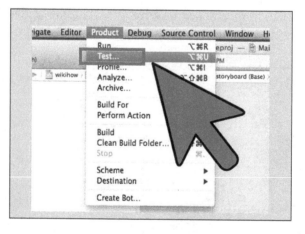

4. Test it over and over. Bugs are the bane of every developer. Errors in code and unexpected usage can cause all kinds of problems in a finished product. As you continue to work on your project, test it as much as possible. Do everything you can to break it, and then try to keep it from breaking in the future. Have friends and family test your program and report back results. Any way that you can get feedback will help your development process.

- Try inputting odd dates if your program deals with dates. Really old dates or far future dates may cause odd reactions with the program.

- Input the wrong kind of variables. For example, if you have a form that asks for the user's age, enter in a word instead and see what happens to the program.

- If your program has a graphical interface, click on everything. What happens when you go back to a previous screen, or click buttons in the wrong order?

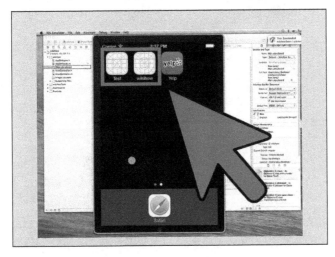

5. Polish your projects. While it's fine to make a rough project for the prototyping and development phase, if you want others to use it you're going to need to spend some time on polish. This means making sure the menus flow logically, the User Interface (UI) is clean and easy to use, there are no glaring or showstopping bugs, and that it's coated in a nice looking finish.

- UI design and functionality can be very difficult and complex. People make whole careers out of designing UIs. Just make sure that your personal project is easy to use and easy on the eyes. A professional UI may not be possible without a budget and a team.

- If you have the budget, there are lots of freelance graphics designers who could potentially design a UI on contract for you. If you have a solid project that you're hoping will become the next big thing, find a good UI designer and make them part of your team.

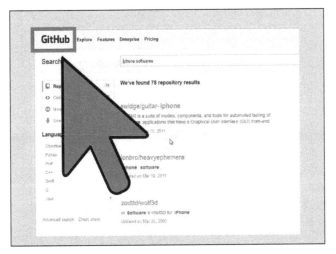

6. Put your projects on GitHub. GitHub is an open-source community that allows you to share your code with others. This will allow you to get insight on your own code as well as benefit others who are looking for solutions that you may have come up with. GitHub is a great learning resource as well as a good way to build your portfolio.

7. Distribute your software. Once you have a finished product, you can choose whether or not you want to distribute it. There are a variety of ways you can do this these days depending on the type of software you created.

- One of the most common ways for small teams or independent developers to distribute their software is through a personal website. Make sure that all of your features are well-documented, and include some screenshots and tutorials. If you are selling your software, make sure you have a good digital payment system and a server to distribute the software from.

- If you are developing software for a specific device or operating system, there are multiple digital stores that you may be able to use. For example, if you are making software for Android devices, you can sell your app through the Google Play Store, the Amazon App Store, or your own personal website.

Part 3. Getting Work

1. Take contract jobs. Although these won't pay as well and are less reliable than full-time employment, you can significantly bulk up your portfolio by taking a series of contract jobs. Check sites like Elance and ODesk (Also known as "Upwork" now) to find work. While it can be difficult to get considered for a contract, once you get your first one it gets a lot easier.

- Hacker News is a great resource for contract and freelance jobs. Check the "Ask" section.

- While it can be tempting to bid low to secure a contract job, don't sell your services short. Not only will you end up working more for less than you deserve, you will also anger others in your field, leading to less networking.

- Good work on a contract job can sometimes lead to a full-time position. Always put your best foot forward.

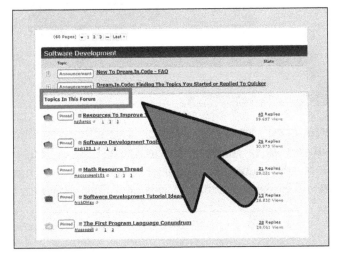

2. Network as much as possible. Attend as many conventions and hack-a-thons as you possibly can. Not only will this expose you to more code and problems to solve, it will also help you meet other people in the industry. Despite what you might think about programmers working alone in their basement, the majority of full-time developers are part of a team and networking is just as important as any other field.

3. Apply for full-time positions. Once you have a few contract jobs under your belt, you can start sending your resume and portfolio out to larger organizations for full-time employment. Besides Monster and Indeed, there are a variety of developer-specific job sites that you should be looking at, including GitHub Jobs, StackOverflow Job Board, AngelList, CrunchBoard, Hirelite, and Hacker News.

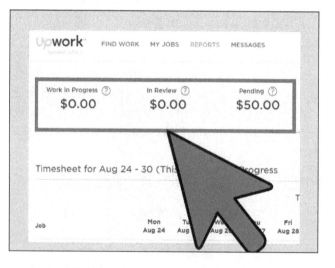

4. Diversify your skillset. A good software developer is usually proficient in more than one language. While a lot of what you learn will be on the job, use some of your free time to expand your knowledge and learn the basics of another language or two. This will make transitioning to new projects much easier and will make you a much more desirable job candidate.

5. Don't worry about the pay. Not every entry-level software development job is going to pay six figures. In fact, none of them will. The good thing about software development, however, is that the job market is incredibly strong. If you feel like you aren't earning enough where you're at, it is relatively easy to move to a new position in a new company (if you have the skills). Treat your first few jobs as necessary experience instead of focusing on your retirement plan.

How to Program Software

Do you have a perfect idea for a program, but don't know how to turn it into a reality? Learning a programming language takes time, but many successful programmers are self-taught. Once you have the basics down, you can create simple programs with minimal time invested. Creating complex programs will be a bit trickier, but with practice, you can be creating your dream program before you know it.

Part 1. Learning a Programming Language

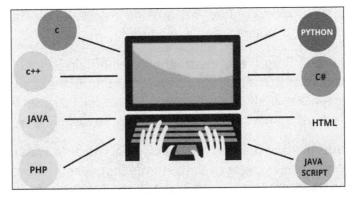

1. Decide on a starting language. If you've never coded before, you'll want to start with a language that is geared towards beginners, but still lets you work towards accomplishing your goals with your program. There are dozens of languages to choose from, and all excel at different tasks and implementations. Some of the most popular languages for new developers include:

- C - One of the older computer languages, but still widely-used. Learning C will also give you a leg up when you expand to C++ and Java.

- C++ - One of the most popular languages in use today, especially in software development. Learning C++ will take a while, and mastering it even longer, but there are countless opportunities once you know it.

- Java - Another incredibly popular language that can be scaled to work on nearly any operating system.

- Python - This is one of the simpler languages in use, and the basics can be learned in just a couple days. It is still quite powerful, and used in a lot of server and website applications.

2. Set up a development environment. You will need a few tools in order to start writing code. These tools are referred to as your "development environment". What you will need varies depending on the language you are coding.

- Code editor - Nearly all programmers will benefit from having a dedicated code editor installed. While you can write code using a simple text editor like Notepad, you'll find the process much easier if you have a program that highlights syntax and automates a lot of the repetitive programming tasks. Some popular code editors include Notepad++, TextMate, and JEdit.

- Compiler or interpreter - Many languages, such as C and Java, need to be compiled before you can execute the code. You will need a compiler for your chosen language installed on your computer. Most compilers will also perform bug-reporting duties.

- IDE (Integrated Development Environment) - Some programming languages have a code editor, compiler, and error-catcher all integrated into one program called an IDE. You can usually get this IDE from the programming language's website.

3. Complete some tutorials. If you've never programmed before, you're going to need to start small. Find some tutorials online that can walk you through the basic concepts of your chosen language. This could include learning about syntax, variables, functions, routines, conditional statements, and how they all fit together.

- There are a variety of places online that provide good tutorials, including Udemy, Khan Academy, Codecademy, Code.org, and many more.

4. Download some sample and open-source programs. Manipulating sample code can help you learn how to perform tasks using that language. There are countless sample and open-source programs available that let you access all of the code that makes the program work. Start with simple programs that are related to the kind of programs you want to make.

5. Create simple programs to learn the basics. When it comes time to start writing your own code, start with the basics. Write a few programs with simple inputs and outputs. Practice techniques you'll need with more complex programs, such as data handling and subroutines. Experiment and try to break your own programs.

6. Join coding communities. Being able to talk to a knowledgeable programmer about any issues you have is invaluable. You can find countless like-minded programmers on various sites and communities around the internet. Join a few related to your chosen language and read everything you can. Don't be afraid to ask questions, but be sure that you've tried to come up with a solution on your own first.

7. Understand that learning any programming language takes time. You won't be able to make a program the first time you sit down at your keyboard (not a complex program, anyway). Learning how to use the programming language effectively takes time, but with practice you'll soon be coding much faster and more efficiently.

Part 2. Designing Your Program

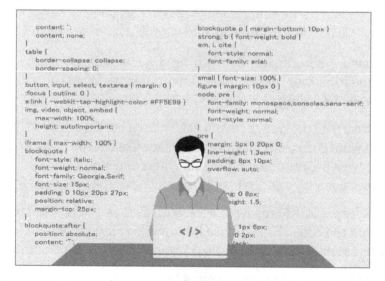

1. Write up a basic design document. Before you start coding your program, it will help to have some written material to refer to during the programming process. The design document outlines

the goals of the program and describes the features in depth. This allows you to stay focused on the function the program.

- The design document should discuss each of the features you want to include and how they will be implemented.

- The design document should also consider the user experience flow and how the user accomplishes his or her task using the program.

2. Map out the program using rough sketches. Create a map for your program, indicating how the user gets from one part to another. A simple flowchart is usually perfectly fine for a basic program.

3. Determine the underlying architecture of the program you are creating. The goals of the program will dictate the structure that you pick. Knowing which one of the following structures best relates to your program will help focus the development.

4. Start with a "1-2-3" program. This is the most simple type of program, and allows you to get comfortable with your programming language. Basically, a 1-2-3 program starts, asks for input from the user, and then displays a result. After the result is displayed, the program ends.

- The next step after a 1-2-3 is a REPL (Read-Execute-Print Loop). This is a 1-2-3 program that goes back to 1 after displaying the output.

- Consider a Pipeline program. This is a program that transforms user input and runs continuously. This is a method good for programs that require little user interaction, such as an RSS reader. The program will be written as a series of classes that share a loop.

Part 3. Creating a Prototype

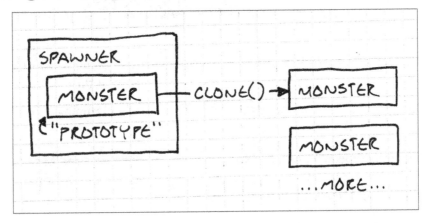

1. Focus on one feature. A prototype usually focuses on the main feature of the program. For example, if you're creating a personal organizer program, your prototype may be the calendar and event-adding function.

2. Iterate until the feature works. Your prototype should be able to be used as its own program. It will be the foundation of everything else, so make sure its working properly. As you iterate on the feature, continue to refine it until it works smoothly and efficiently.

- The prototype allows you to make rapid changes and then test them out.

- Have others test your prototype to ensure that it functions properly.

- Expect the prototype to change as you work on it.

3. Don't be afraid to scrap the prototype. The whole point of the prototype is to experiment before committing. The prototype allows you to see if the features you want are possible before you dive into coding the program proper. If the prototype is doomed to fail, scrap it and return to the drawing board. It will save you a lot of headache down the line.

Part 4. Making the Program

1. Create a pseudocode base. This is the skeleton for your project, and will serve as the base for future coding. Pseudo-code is similar to code but won't actually compile. Instead, it allows programmers to read and parse what is supposed to be happening with the code.

- Pseudo-code still refers to the syntax of the programming language, and the pseudo-code should be structured just like regular code would be.

2. Expand on your prototype. You can use your existing prototype as the base for your new program, or you can adapt the prototype code into the larger structure of your full program. In either case, make good use of the time that you spent working on and refining the prototype.

3. Start coding. This is the real meat of the process. Coding will take the longest time, and will require numerous compiles and tests to ensure that the code works. If you are working with a team, starting from pseudo-code can help keep everyone on the same page.

4. Comment on all of your code. Use your programming language's comment feature to add comment to all of your code. Not only will this help anyone who works on your program figure out what the code does, but it will also help you remember what your own code does when you come back to the project later.

Part 5. Testing the Program

1. Test every new feature. Every new feature added to the program should be compiled and tested. The more people that you can get to test, the more likely that you'll be able to spot errors. Your testers should be made aware that the program is far from final and that they can and will encounter serious errors.

- This is often referred to as alpha testing.

2. Test your feature-complete program. Once you've implemented all of the features in your program, you should begin a round of intensive testing that covers all aspects of the program. This round of testing should also include the largest number of testers yet.

- This is often referred to as beta testing.

3. Test the release candidate. As you continue to make adjustments and add assets to your program, make sure that the version you intend to release has been thoroughly tested.

Part 6. Creating Assets

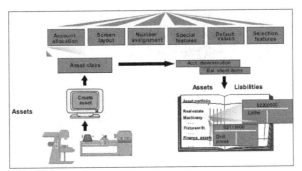

1. Determine what you'll need. The nature of the program will determine the assets you will need. Do you need custom sounds? Artwork? Content? All of these questions should be answered before you release your program.

2. Consider outsourcing. If you need a lot of assets, but don't have the manpower or talent to create them yourself, you can consider outsourcing asset creation. There are countless freelancers out there that may be willing to work on your project.

3. Implement your assets. Make sure that they do not interfere with the functionality of your program, and that there is nothing superfluous. Adding assets usually occurs int eh final stages of the programming cycle, unless the assets are integral to the program itself. This is most often the case in video game programming.

Part 7. Releasing the Program

1. Consider releasing your programs as open-source. This allows others to take the code you've made and improve on it. Open-source is a community-driven model of releasing, and you will likely see little profit. The benefits are that other programmers could take interest in your project and help expand the scope significantly.

2. Create a storefront. If you want to sell your software, you can create a storefront on your website to allow customers to buy and download your software. Keep in mind that if you have paying customers, they will expect a working and error-free product.

- Depending on your product, there are a variety of services that you can sell it through as well.

3. Keep supporting your release. After releasing your software, you will likely start receiving bug reports from new users. Categorize these bugs by their critical levels, and then start tackling them. As you update the program, you can release new versions or patches that update specific parts of the code.

- Strong post-release support can increase your customer retention and spread good word of mouth.

4. Advertise your software. People will need to know your software exists before they start using it. Give out review copies to relevant review sites, consider creating a free trial version, write a press release, and do everything you can to spread the word about your software.

Software Consultant

A software consultant is a professional who assesses a business or organization's processes and provides software solutions and other recommendations based on that assessment. This professional may perform this function either as a self-employed individual, or as part of a software consulting firm. He or she may integrate customized software into a business or organization's processes in order to increase efficiency and minimize manpower or costs.

For example, a gym or fitness center could benefit from the integration of proprietary software that tracks the progress of the gym's members, in the form of measurements and other personalized data. A consultant, either individually or as part of a firm, might specialize in the creation of such a software for fitness centers, and pitch the software to various business and organizations within the fitness industry.

As software can perform a wide variety of functions, a software consultant might deliver software solutions to a wide variety of industries. Businesses and organizations will often hire one or a firm on a contract basis, if such expertise is not already be available in-house. For example, a real estate company that already employs a computer programmer, webmaster, or other information technology (IT) professionals might also hire a consultant who can create a database of properties customized to suit the company's information management needs.

Software consulting firms that are contracted by businesses or organizations are often hired on a project basis. This means the consulting firm must integrate new software into the business or organization within a certain time frame agreed-upon by both parties. The project team, which is typically made up of personnel from both the hirer's organization and the software consulting firm, work together to come up with software solutions that suits the needs of the business or organization. Personnel who will work closely with the software often receive special training during the project and are heavily-involved in its integration to help familiarize them with its various functions.

As businesses and organizations have become increasingly reliant on technology, the development of new and improved software systems delivered by a software consultant can sometimes render certain positions or expenses obsolete. For example, software can be programmed to analyze patterns in various data, retrieve specific information within a variety of parameters, and eliminate the need for hard copy storage, such as filing rooms and various filing systems. In such a case, the business or organization may no longer require a filing clerk or filing supplies and storage.

How to Become a Software Consultant

If you are a self-starter who likes problem solving and logical thinking, being a software consultant could be the right career choice. The finance, government, automotive, and aerospace sectors rely on software consultants to give them technical advice. Consultants advise clients on how to configure large applications, write code, or fix bugs. They customize software systems for specific tasks or industries. Software consultants also analyze company computer systems to determine how software can make processes more efficient. To be a software consultant, you should acquire the necessary education or training, market yourself effectively, and solicit clientele.

Part 1. Acquiring Education and Work Experience

1. Learn about software engineering, software development, web design, and troubleshooting. Mastering the fundamentals of software engineering will help you see if this career is the right fit. One option is to obtain a Bachelor of Software Engineering (B.SE.) at an ABET accredited college or university. You also could teach yourself from books, online tutorials, and/or trial and error. Some students obtain masters degrees in software engineering as well.

- Many software engineering degree programs require that applicants have taken advanced computer science and math courses in high school. If you have finished high school and did not take these courses, enroll in a community college to gather necessary credits.

- Read software engineering blogs to stay informed with developments in the field.

2. Seek an internship or part-time job in software engineering. During your studies or self-education time, gain practical experience through employment. Use university resources to perfect your resume. Attend career fairs to discuss software engineering jobs with technology sector employees.

3. Acquire your first software engineering job. Apply for entry-level jobs in software engineering to prepare to become a consultant. During this time, you should work towards earning your engineering license. To receive your license, you must pass the Fundamentals of Engineering exam. You can take the exam after four to six years of employment.

- Upon receiving your engineering license, you should understand the foundations of software engineering, development, and troubleshooting. You should have programming skills in programming languages like C++, Java, HTML, SQL, Perl, Falcon, Lynx, and Matlab.

Part 2. Developing your Specialty

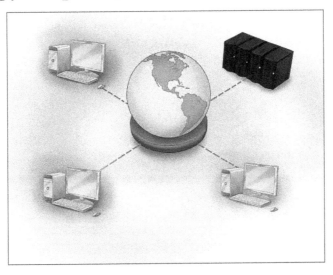

1. Find your niche. Within software consulting, find your area of specialization so you can offer something specific to customers. If you find a particular area of software engineering that interests you, you are more likely to enjoy work. Pick a specialization in, for example, cyber security, networking, or systems engineering. Research which software consulting services are available near you and what is lacking.

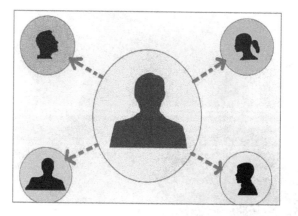

2. Network with other software engineers. Attend conferences and networking events with other software engineers to build connections. Pay particular attention to experts working in your specialty. Attend experts' conference lectures and try to meet them afterwards. Ask the experts and your colleagues for blog recommendations and/or advice.

3. Develop your own software in your specialty. You might create an application for a smartphone or something more advanced like internet security software. Do multiple trials and work out any kinks. By developing and perfecting your own product, you will have a finished project to show to prospective clients.

Part 3. Launching your Consultancy

1. Set up your business. When your software is complete and you are ready to begin consulting, develop your company name and logo. Use these items in your marketing materials. Set your hourly

rate and create a billing system. Do market research to see what others charge in your geographic and expertise areas. In determining your rate, also consider your expenses.

- As you gain expertise, you can adjust your billing rates. Be sure to raise rates at convenient times for clients, such as the end of the fiscal or calendar years. Be transparent about any rate changes.

2. Market your software and consulting services. Create brochures, a website, and business cards. Advertise how your skills, experience, and education can help a company. Demonstrate why your software is better or how it compares to other software. It will take time to build your client list. Consider keeping your full-time job at first to ensure a steady income. Once you have clients, your expertise, communication style, and business communications will develop further.

- Explain that you have software for sale and offer services as a consultant in your area of expertise. If you can do troubleshooting or write code, specify that as well. Include this information on your business cards.

- Think about offering company-wide or online seminars and how-to tutorials. You want to seem approachable and knowledgeable. Attendees also might ask you to work for them or give your name to others.

3. Broadcast your success. With client permission, advertise completed projects. Use conference papers, a blog, and/or a website to publicize your work. Utilize social media websites, like Facebook or Twitter, to advertise and to write posts about your successes.

- Ask satisfied clients to recommend you to colleagues or friends. By using the snowball effect, your business should grow quickly.

Part 4. Succeeding as a Software Consultant

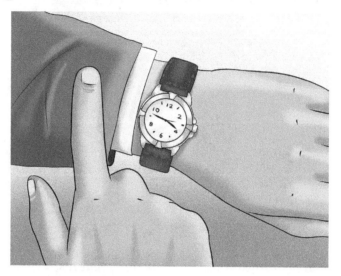

1. Practice good time management. If you remain self-employed and independent, your schedule will be more flexible. Track hours and plan days ahead to ensure that you complete work in a timely, efficient manner. Schedule hours for phone calls, client meetings, and networking events.

2. Manage your finances. Consider hiring a Certified Public Accountant (CPA). As an independent contractor, your tax situation will be more complicated than if you were an employee. If you live in the U.S., you must pay full social security contributions and purchase health insurance. Plan to contribute money to a private pension plan. Consider purchasing professional liability insurance to protect you in the case of a client lawsuit.

- If you have a spouse with health insurance, you might avoid needing to purchase insurance.

3. Continue networking. Within the software consulting industry, who you know is vastly important. Some consultants spend ten hours a week connecting with new contacts and maintaining past relationships. Be willing to help consultants who have less experience than you.

Software Engineers

A software engineer is a licensed professional engineer who is schooled and skilled in the application of engineering discipline to the creation of software.

Engineering Code of Ethics and License

A software engineer is often confused with a programmer, but the two are vastly different disciplines. A programmer is tasked with creating the code that makes a program run, whereas a software engineer is responsible for designing, developing and implementing the software solutions programmers create.

By U.S. law no person may use the title "engineer" (of any type) unless the person holds a professional engineering license from a state licensing board and is in good standing with the board. A software engineer is also held accountable to a specific code of ethics.

Software Engineer Job Description and Requirements

The role of a software engineer, or computer software engineer, is to develop highly functional, solution-based software processes and solutions that address specific needs within an organization or department. These software solutions need to have been thoroughly tested for accuracy and security before implementation, and they need to comply with current coding standards and operating procedures.

Software engineers are tasked with evaluating existing operations within the company, finding and defining problems or areas for improvement, proposing and developing solutions for these issues in the form of new or improved software processes, and testing, implementing, and maintaining these software changes.

This requires in-depth knowledge and experience with the software development lifecycle (SDLC) and the ability to write and explain code created in a variety of languages such as C++, .NET, Java, Python, etc. A software engineer needs to be able to communicate at both a very in-depth, detailed level with computer programmers as well as a broader "big picture" level with IT managers and upper management.

What Does a Software Engineer Do in a Typical Day

A software engineer's typical work day involves juggling a variety of tasks and balancing working on numerous software projects that are often in different stages of the software development lifecycle (SDLC). Meetings to discuss software project status updates, new software project roadmaps, and organizational logistics such as new hires also play a key role in a software engineer's workweek.

Software engineers are expected to prioritize their tasks while working on several software projects in parallel, and as a result their work day might involve writing or refining software code for one project in the morning before attending or running a meeting to cover the progress on another software project, followed by conceptualizing and developing ideas and requirements for an upcoming project, before finally wrapping up the day by documenting milestones and progress made over the course of the day or week.

Because a software engineer is expected to be able to balance numerous tasks as well as be able to tackle problems at both a deep, code-based level as well as a broad, "big picture" level, a computer software engineer's work regularly involves:

- Analyzing spreadsheets and reports to identify performance bottlenecks, operational issues, and other areas for improvement.

- Brainstorming and developing plans, flowcharts, layouts and resource requests as part of creating new software projects as potential solutions for identified issues.

- Write high-quality, well-commented code for new and existing software projects.

- Create software verification plans and initiate quality assurance processes.

- Test and integrate software code and components into existing software systems.

- Fully document software systems and plans for maintaining software projects.

- Ensure compliance with regulations and industry standards.

- Monitor, troubleshoot, debug and improve software code base for existing systems.

- Update and patch software systems as necessary with security patches and feature upgrades.

Education

Half of all practitioners today have degrees in computer science, information systems, or information technology. A small, but growing, number of practitioners have software engineering degrees. In 1987, Imperial College London introduced the first three-year software engineering Bachelor's degree in the UK and the world; in the following year, the University of Sheffield established a similar program. In 1996, the Rochester Institute of Technology established the first software engineering bachelor's degree program in the United States, however, it did not obtain ABET accreditation until 2003, the same time as Rice University, Clarkson University, Milwaukee School of Engineering and Mississippi State University obtained theirs. In 1997, PSG College of Technology in Coimbatore, India was the first to start a five-year integrated Master of Science degree in Software Engineering.

Since then, software engineering undergraduate degrees have been established at many universities. A standard international curriculum for undergraduate software engineering degrees was recently[when?] defined by the CCSE. As of 2004, in the U.S., about 50 universities offer software engineering degrees, which teach both computer science and engineering principles and practices. The first software engineering Master's degree was established at Seattle University in 1979. Since then graduate software engineering degrees have been made available from many more universities. Likewise in Canada, the Canadian Engineering Accreditation Board (CEAB) of the Canadian Council of Professional Engineers has recognized several software engineering programs.

In 1998, the US Naval Postgraduate School (NPS) established the first doctorate program in Software Engineering in the world. Additionally, many online advanced degrees in Software Engineering have appeared such as the Master of Science in Software Engineering (MSE) degree offered through the Computer Science and Engineering Department at California State University, Fullerton. Steve McConnell opines that because most universities teach computer science rather than software engineering, there is a shortage of true software engineers. ETS University and UQAM (Université du Québec à Montréal) were mandated by IEEE to develop the Software Engineering Body of Knowledge (SWEBOK), which has become an ISO standard describing the body of knowledge covered by a software engineer.

Other Degrees

In business, some software engineering practitioners have MIS or computer information systems degrees. In embedded systems, some have electrical engineering, electronics engineering, computer science with emphasis in "embedded systems" or computer engineering degrees, because embedded software often requires a detailed understanding of hardware. In medical software, practitioners may have medical informatics, general medical, or biology degrees.

Some practitioners have mathematics, science, engineering, or technology (STEM) degrees. Some have philosophy (logic in particular) or other non-technical degrees. For instance, Barry Boehm earned degrees in mathematics. And, others have no degrees.

Profession

Employment

Most software engineers work as employees or contractors. Software engineers work with businesses, government agencies (civilian or military), and non-profit organizations. Some software engineers work on their own as consulting software engineers. Some organizations have specialists to perform all of the tasks in the software development process. Other organizations separate software engineers based on specific software-engineering tasks. These companies sometimes hire interns (possibly university or college students) over a short time. In large projects, software engineers are distinguished from people who specialize in only one role because they take part in the design as well as the programming of the project. In small projects, software engineers will usually fill several or all roles at the same time. Specializations include:

- In industry (analysts, architects, developers, testers, technical support, managers)

- In academia (educators, researchers).

There is considerable debate over the future employment prospects for Software Engineers and other IT Professionals. For example, an online futures market called the Future of IT Jobs in America attempted to answer whether there would be more IT jobs, including software engineers, in 2012 than there were in 2002. Possible opportunities for advancement can be as a Software Engineer, then to a Senior Software Engineer, or straight to a Senior Software Engineer, depending on skills and reputation. Services exist that are trying to better gauge the coding ability of an engineer, given not all engineers progress their abilities at the same rate, and to make it easier for both employers and employees to find a good match in terms of jobs.

Software developers working in academia in the UK have founded and fostered the concept of a "Research Software Engineer" (RSE).

Work

This job is office-based, and most of the work is done during normal office hours, but can sometimes lead to working away and working late or during weekends, depending on where and when the client is situated. The job can also be done at home or anywhere a computer is set up.

Impact of Globalization

Most students in the developed world have avoided degrees related to software engineering because of the fear of offshore outsourcing (importing software products or services from other countries) and of being displaced by foreign visa workers. Although government statistics do not currently show a threat to software engineering itself; a related career, computer programming does appear to have been affected. Often one is expected to start out as a computer programmer before being promoted to software engineer. Thus, the career path to software engineering may be rough, especially during recessions.

Some career counselors suggest a student also focus on "people skills" and business skills rather than purely technical skills because such "soft skills" are allegedly more difficult to offshore. Reasonable command over reading, writing & speaking English is asked by most of employers. It is the quasi-management aspects of software engineering that appear to be what has kept it from being impacted by globalization.

Prizes

There are several prizes in the field of software engineering:

- The Codie awards is a yearly award issued by the Software and Information Industry Association for excellence in software development within the software industry.
- Jolt Awards are awards in the software industry.
- Stevens Award is a software engineering award given in memory of Wayne Stevens.

Origin of the Term

Margaret Hamilton promoted the term "software engineering" during her work on the Apollo program. The term "engineering" was used to acknowledge that the work should be taken just as seriously as other contributions toward the advancement of technology. Hamilton details her use of the term:

> When I first came up with the term, no one had heard of it before, at least in our world. It was an ongoing joke for a long time. They liked to kid me about my radical ideas. It was a memorable day when one of the most respected hardware gurus explained to everyone in a meeting that he agreed with me that the process of building software should also be considered an engineering discipline, just like with hardware. Not because of his acceptance of the new "term" per se, but because we had earned his and the acceptance of the others in the room as being in an engineering field in its own right.

Suitability of the Term

One could argue that software engineering implies a certain level of academic training, professional discipline, adherence to formal processes, and especially legal liability that often are not applied in cases of software development. A common analogy is that working in construction does not make one a civil engineer, and so writing code does not make one a software engineer. Furthermore, because computing doesn't utilize the methods of mathematical physics common to all conventional engineering disciplines, it is more appropriate to call those engaged in this occupation as software developers or similar.

In 1978, computer scientist E. W. Dijkstra wrote in a paper that the coining of the term software engineer was not useful since it was an inappropriate analogy:

> The existence of the mere term has been the base of a number of extremely shallow—and false—analogies, which just confuse the issue. Computers are such exceptional gadgets that there is good reason to assume that most analogies with other disciplines are too shallow to be of any positive value, are even so shallow that they are only confusing.

In each of the last few decades, at least one radical new approach has entered the mainstream of software development (e.g. Structured Programming, Object Orientation), implying that the field is still changing too rapidly to be considered an engineering discipline. Proponents argue that the supposedly radical new approaches are evolutionary rather than revolutionary.

Individual commentators have disagreed sharply on how to define software engineering or its legitimacy as an engineering discipline. David Parnas has said that software engineering is, in fact, a form of engineering. Steve McConnell has said that it is not, but that it should be. Donald Knuth has said that programming is an art and a science. Edsger W. Dijkstra claimed that the terms software engineering and software engineer have been misused and should be considered harmful, particularly in the United States.

Regulatory Classification

Canada

In Canada the use of the job title Engineer is controlled in each province by self-regulating professional engineering organizations who are also tasked with enforcement of the governing legislation. The intent is that any individual holding themselves out as an engineer has been verified to have been educated to a certain accredited level and their professional practice is subject to a code of ethics and peer scrutiny. It is also illegal to use the title Engineer in Canada unless an individual is licensed.

In Ontario, the Professional Engineers Act stipulates a minimum education level of a three-year diploma in technology from a College of Applied Arts and Technology or a degree in a relevant science area. However, engineering undergraduates and all other applicants are not allowed to use the title of engineer until they complete the minimum amount of work experience of four years in addition to completing the Professional Practice Examination (PPE). If the applicant does not hold an undergraduate engineering degree then they may have to take the Confirmatory Practice Exam or Specific Examination Program unless the exam requirements are waived by a committee.

IT professionals with degrees in other fields (such as computer science or information systems) are restricted from using the title Software Engineer, or wording Software Engineer in a title, depending on their province or territory of residence.

In some instances, cases have been taken to court regarding the illegal use of the protected title Engineer.

France

In France, the term ingénieur (engineer) is not a protected title and can be used by anyone, even by those who do not possess an academic degree.

However, the title Ingénieur Diplomé (Graduate Engineer) is an official academic title that is protected by the government and is associated with the Diplôme d'Ingénieur, which is one of the most prestigious academic degrees in France.

Iceland

The use of the title tölvunarfræðingur (computer scientist) is protected by law in Iceland. Software engineering is taught in Computer Science departments in Icelandic universities. Icelandic law state that a permission must be obtained from the Minister of Industry when the degree was awarded abroad, prior to use of the title. The title is awarded to those who have obtained a BSc degree in Computer Science from a recognized higher educational institution.

New Zealand

In New Zealand, the Institution of Professional Engineers New Zealand (IPENZ), which licenses and regulates the country's chartered engineers (CPEng), recognizes software engineering as a legitimate branch of professional engineering and accepts application of software engineers to obtain chartered status provided he or she has a tertiary degree of approved subjects. Software Engineering is included whereas Computer Science is normally not.

United States

The Bureau of Labor Statistics (BLS) classifies computer software engineers as a subcategory of "computer specialists", along with occupations such as computer scientist, Programmer, Database administrator and Network administrator. The BLS classifies all other engineering disciplines, including computer hardware engineers, as engineers.

Many states prohibit unlicensed persons from calling themselves an Engineer, or from indicating branches or specialties not covered licensing acts. In many states, the title Engineer is reserved for individuals with a Professional Engineering license indicating that they have shown minimum level of competency through accredited engineering education, qualified engineering experience, and engineering board's examinations.

In April 2013 the National Council of Examiners for Engineering and Surveying (NCEES) began offering a Professional Engineer (PE) exam for Software Engineering. The exam was developed in association with the IEEE Computer Society. NCEES will end the exam after April 2019 due to lack of participation.

How to Become a Software Engineers

Method 1. Entering Software Engineering as your First Career

1. Earn a degree in computer science or a related field. Most software engineer positions require a bachelor's degree. Majoring in computer science will provide the most useful background for designing and perfecting software. Most often, interviewers will ask questions focusing on data structures and algorithms, so the theoretical background provided by traditional computer science degrees best prepares you for this. However, you will likely need to spend considerable time outside of the classroom writing software to learn how the theoretical concepts you're taught can apply in the practice of writing real software.

- It is possible to get hired with an associate's degree or even with nothing but self-taught experience. Pursuing this route, you should have a strong collection of completed and functional projects demonstrating your skills on a website like Github. You can also pursue open source projects to contribute fixes and new features to in case you don't have a concept of your own. Open source means that the code (source) for a piece of software is publicly viewable (open). Often, this allows anyone to submit code to a project, pending approval of the project maintainers. Finding an open source project with a welcoming community of developers can greatly accelerate your skills after you've established a baseline skillset.

2. Begin programming. Even if you're still in grade school, you can give yourself a huge head start by teaching yourself programming.

- Software engineering is not focused exclusively on coding, but you will need to know at least a couple languages, and a deeper understanding of how they function. There is no widespread agreement on which languages are most useful, but these are all popular choices:

  - Python

  - Ruby

  - JavaScript

  - C#

  - Java

  - C++

- Be aware that some languages are better at solving some problems than others. No one language is better than another. No one language is objectively easier than another. Most languages were written with certain types of problems in mind and are better at solving them while weaker at solving others. Experiment and get a feel for your style. At first, only focus on getting the most basic of programs running in one language. Once you've gotten comfortable with one, start experimenting with a second. There is no need to learn all languages. Find your niche and become awesome at it.

- For youth, MIT (Massachusetts Institute of Technology) created the website and programming tool, Scratch. This tool teaches programming concepts using visual queues rather than intimidating text. It's also useful to adults who would feel more comfortable focusing on visual elements rather than abstract concepts and text.

3. Study data structures and algorithms. "Algorithm" simply means a formula or process for solving a problem. Common examples are path-finding for finding the shortest distance between two points, searching for finding a specific item of data in a large set of data, and sorting for arranging data in some order. A "data structure" is a certain way of organizing data to make it easier to solve certain problems. Common examples are arrays that simply contain items of data one after anoth-

er in some order and hash tables that store data by some "key" instead of a position in a list. Focus on developing and maintaining your skills in order to do your best once you've obtained a position as a software engineer.

- (Optional) Study math. Mathematics will be a part of any computer science major, and many algorithms and data structures knowledge stems from mathematics. While not absolutely necessary, having a strong background in math will give you stronger core skills for analyzing and designing new algorithms. If you're targeting companies that do cutting-edge research and development, math will be a must. If you want a cushy corporate job, you can likely skim through higher level math.

- Discrete mathematics is a particularly useful area of study, as is any math course that involves software.

4. Supplement your studies. Educational systems are often outdated. Textbooks are revised slower than software is updated. Educational institutions provide theoretical concepts and ways of thinking that can be critical to your success, and therefore should not be discounted. However, what will get you paid is being able to apply the theory to real-world software. This is where supplementing your studies comes in.

- Browse through StackOverflow. StackOverflow is a question and answer website for developers. You can search by tag to identify the technology, problem space, or language you want to improve in. Seeing others' answers will give you insight into how engineers solve problems. Bookmarking clever solutions will also help you build your problem-solving toolkit.

- Use practice sites for coding. Sites like CodeWars and CodinGame offer thousands of problems for you to test your skills against.

- Find a real-world community to help keep you inspired, develop connections, and give you guidance on where to focus your learning. Sites like Meetup can be great places to find software engineers and learn more about the profession. If you have trouble finding general engineering meetups, try to focus on specific languages or technologies. Check out social media sites, as well.

5. Build software. The best way to improve your skills is to use them. Whether professional projects or personal, designing and coding software will teach you a great deal. For many employers, hands-on achievements matter more than GPA or theoretical knowledge.

- Unless you plan on monetizing the software you build, put it online. Allowing potential employers to see the projects you've created and the code powering them allows them to assess your skills. It's also a great way to get feedback to help improve your skills.

6. Seek an internship. Many software engineer students work as interns while they complete their studies. This can be an excellent way to gain hands-on training and network with potential employers. Look for internship opportunities through job posting websites and networking.

7. Find job opportunities. Software engineering is a rapidly growing field. You have a good chance of immediate employment, although you may start as a programmer and work your way up to software development. Start searching before your degree is up:

- Colleges often help their alumni obtain a position. Talk to your professors, department staff, and the career services office about finding job opportunities.

- A large percentage of jobs happen through networking. Use your personal contacts, and meet people in the field through career meet ups and conferences.

- Check job search websites regularly. Create a profile and post your resume to professional sites and use them for networking as well as job applications.

8. Consider your career goals. The software industry is always changing. Keep up by improving your knowledge and practical skills, and you'll have many chances to shape the direction of your career. Here are a few ways to improve your job prospects:

- Join a professional organization for networking opportunities.

- Consider a Master's degree if you have long-term plans in the field. While not a requirement for most positions, a Master's greatly improves your chances to work for an industry leader, in a management position, or in embedded software. A Master's degree can also give you a considerable pay bump early in your career.

- Certification can be useful in some sub-fields and regions, but may decrease your desirability in others. Talk to other engineers in your area of expertise before you enroll in one of these programs. Often, traditional corporate environments favor certificates, but start-ups and highly progressive companies can find them as a waste of time. However, there are always exceptions. Some countries also view certificates differently, so try to connect with software engineers and understand how the industry in your area operates.

Method 2. Switching to a Software Engineer Career

1. Know your job prospects. The software development field has excellent job growth. Software engineering is a particularly desirable focus compared to basic programming. Median software developer income is roughly $80,000 – $100,000 a year in the United States.

2. Learn programming. Practical software design and coding should be your first priorities. There are a variety of ways to earn this experience:

- Teach yourself programming through online tutorials or friends willing to teach you.

- Take a massive open online course (MOOC).

- If you already have some experience, collaborate with other programmers on GitHub.

- A coding bootcamp is one of the fastest ways to learn, if you're willing to invest money and free time. Just make sure to do your research, as some bootcamps have poor reputations in industry and may not be worth the money.

3. Draw on your experience. Software may be a specialized subject, but your previous career doesn't have to involve computers to give you an edge. Software engineering can rely heavily on analytic skills, problem solving, and teamwork. In addition, familiarity with an industry may help you design software for that industry.

- Even hobbies and side interests can open up networking opportunities, or at least add passion to your job. Game apps, digital music suites, or business software are all examples.

- If possible, automate portions of your job. Build tools to speed up tasks and make things easier. Software engineering at its core is problem solving. Writing software is just a software engineer's chosen method of solving problems. There are problems all around you already. There's no reason you can't start now.

4. Enroll in a degree program (optional). It's very possible to land a programming job after a year or two of side experience, or even a few months with enough dedication. If you already have a bachelor's in any subject, along with some coding skills, consider going straight for a master's in software engineering.

- Be aware that this is an incredibly expensive option. However, if you have difficulty being self-motivated and joining a community or trying a hobby doesn't stick, this could be the most effective option.

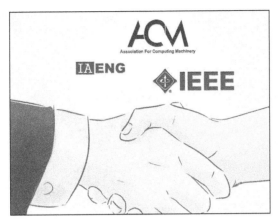

5. Network your way to a job. Almost every industry needs software developers, so your network from a previous career can be invaluable. Also consider joining a professional association, such as IAENG Society of Software Engineering, the IEEE Computer Society Technical Council on Software Engineering, or the Association for Computing Machinery. Also, look into local meetups or online communities. The software world can be surprisingly small, and finding the right connection can open up a myriad of opportunities.

How to Learn to be a Softwar Engineer for free

Acquiring skills in information technology is a smart way to boost your career. Gaining a degree in software engineering can help you to get jobs with excellent pay, or simply bring more skills to your current job. However, not all people are able to return to school to gain this degree. Luckily, there are a few free courses through excellent universities that offer everyone the chance to study software engineering. You will need to be self-disciplined in order to learn this complicated information on your own.

Steps

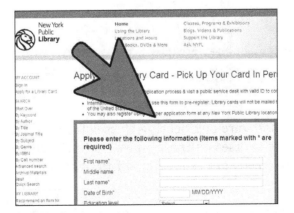

1. Sign up for a library card at your local branch. Checking out or requesting books like "Beginning Programming For Dummies" and "Hello World. Computer Programming for Kids and Other

Beginners" will acquaint you with the terms and options of software engineering. Once you have established some basic knowledge you can request books about specific programs or types of software engineering.

2. Sign up for the Khan Academy. Two Massachusetts Institute of Technology (MIT) graduates started this undergraduate tutorial program to help people learn basic college subjects for free, such as software engineering. Download the iTunes application, watch the tutorial videos and do the practice tests.

- You will not receive credit for the tutorials you take; however, once you have an account, you will be able to track your progress with the classes and practice tests.

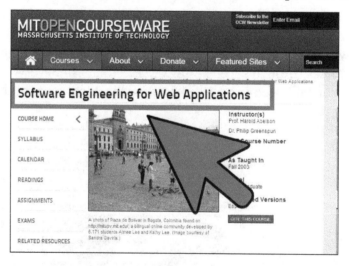

3. Review and take online software engineering classes from MIT Open Courseware. MIT offers certain free engineering courses online. You will not be earning credits; however, you will be getting lectures and materials offered from 1 of the best technological universities in the world.

- Ocw.mit.edu offers courses like "Introduction to Computers and Engineering Problem Solving," "Introduction to Computer Science and Programming," "Computer Science Mathematics," "Computer Language Engineering" and "Computing and Data Analysis."

You may be required to complete prerequisite lower level courses before doing the more advanced options.

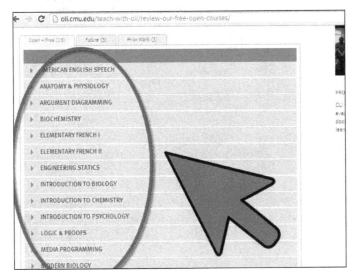

4. Check the Opening Learning Initiative at the Carnegie Melon University. This grant-funded program offers courses like computational mathematics, coding, engineering statistics and other courses that are university-level and applicable to learning software engineering. The course materials and instruction are free; however, you will not receive any credit for taking the class.

- Go to [oli.cmu.edu] to look at a course schedule. Classes change regularly, so you can check in both the open and future class sections.

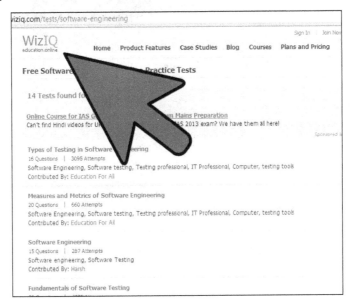

5. Take practice tests at [wiziq.com/tests/software-engineering]. Through this aggregate, you have options to take tests on your skills as you progress. Organizations like Education For All offer practice with software testing, software engineering basics and knowledge in specific software framework.

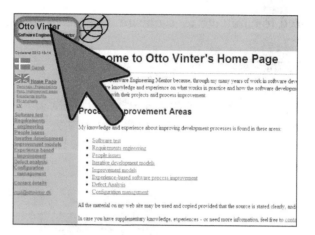

6. Find a software engineering mentor. Contact local software engineers and volunteer some free man hours to learn what they do. You may be able to supplement your education with their practical know-how, while donating hours of programming to their own efforts.

7. Begin working on open source programs. Sites like WordPress and Drupal allow people to create and improve their programs in their spare time. This results in an excellent collaborative effort and extensive programming resources that can help you with your own engineering.

8. Take exams to earn credits if you want to earn a degree. If you want to gain an associate's or bachelor's degree in information technology, you can take the College Board's exams in order to gain

college credit by proving your advanced knowledge. If you receive a high score on these tests, the credits will be accepted at 2/3 of American colleges and universities.

- You can also take exams at Excelsior College in order to gain credits. The exams cost approximately $100 and you can receive 3 to 8 credits. If you pass these exams and transfer credits to a university or college the credits themselves will be inexpensive and you will have fewer courses to pay for while studying for your degree.

How to Interview for a Software Engineer Position

Interviewing for a Software Engineering position has points in common with every other job interview situation, but it also has its peculiarities. This article was written both for the new college graduate and for the experienced engineer.

Steps

1. Understand you're not looking for a job; you're offering your services. Companies aren't interested in giving you a job per se. They have a situation of some kind and want to know if you can provide the solution.

- Sometimes the situation may be, "we're looking for good all-around programming ability"; more often than it's "do you have significant experience with language X (Java, Python, C++) or field Y (CAD, networking, embedded systems)?" Some knowledge in algorithms like big O notation often comes in handy in many cases.

2. Familiarize yourself with the company, what it does, and the products it sells. Think about how you could be an asset to the company.

3. If you know someone who works at the company already, by all means contact them. Knowing some-one at a company means you already have someone who can vouch for you, and is a great advantage.

4. Understand that if you want a specific job, but don't know the language used, you can still get the job. How? By learning the language yourself, and demonstrating your knowledge to the employer.

- If you already know a few languages, one more is usually just variations on a theme. An experienced engineer learning a new language is often more valuable to a company than a recent graduate with a couple of years experience. Doing so also demonstrates self-reli-ance, always a positive trait for an engineer.

5. Many companies these days will screen candidates by phone before inviting them to a face-to-face interview. This saves the company a lot of time, as many candidates who "look good on paper" cannot otherwise answer basic questions.

6. The initial phone screen may be conducted by a non-technical person. They are looking for answers that match the ones they've been given by engineers. They will not understand subtlety, so don't bother with other than straightforward answers.

7. If you pass the first screen (or there isn't one), next comes the engineering screen. Your interviewer will be either the group manager or another engineer. You may be given programming problems to solve over the phone. Have pen and paper ready. Some companies will use on-line whiteboards which you will access from your home computer, and the interviewer will be able to see your code as you write it.

8. In this and all interviews, make sure you understand the question. Repeat it back to the interviewer to make sure you're solving the question that was asked. Ask questions to clarify the parameters of the problem; answer questions succinctly.

9. If you passed the engineering screen (or there wasn't one), the next step will be the in-person interview. Companies often schedule a half-day for a first interview, with the candidate meeting four or five engineers, and possibly the manager, with each meeting running 45-60 minutes.

10. Get a good night's sleep the night before, and eat a good breakfast.

11. Always wear a suit (or similarly conservative dress for a woman) to an interview unless you have been specifically told otherwise. Shine your shoes, brush your teeth, wash your hair, etc., and in general look "properly assembled". Women: no big, dangling earrings, low-cut dresses, or other cocktail-party clothes. In general, the image you present should be of understated competence. The real test, of course, is in the substance of the interview, but you don't want to prejudice the interviewer against you to start with.

12. Be on time for the interview, or a few minutes early. Better to get there 45 minutes ahead of time and listen to your car radio for 40 minutes, than to get there 15 minutes late. First impressions count.

13. The person you will meet first is often someone from Human Resources. They may give you an overview of your interview schedule, and may even (if you're lucky) coach you a bit about what's to come. They will then hand you off to your first interviewer.

14. During your interviews, try to be emotionally centered and relaxed. Listen carefully to questions, answer succinctly, and don't jump the gun.

15. Programming questions tend to start off easy and get harder as you progress. Explain your reasoning as you go, and always make sure you're answering the question asked. Ask questions if you need to. If you get really stuck, ask for a hint.

16. Architecture and design questions tend to be naturally looser, and imaginative solutions count for a lot. Try to strike a balance between generality and specificity.

17. Some questions may involve solving logic puzzles that aren't programming-specific. Again, make sure you understand the question correctly before proceeding, and, without rambling, let the interviewer know your thought process. Questions of this kind are often about understanding how you approach problems as much as they are about finding the right answer.

18. If you're given a question already asked by a previous interviewer at the company, inform them of that immediately. They may be testing your honesty.

19. It's OK to say "I don't know" to an interviewer's question, but you should never leave it at that. Ask more questions if they may help you get to an answer, or otherwise explain how you would find information to answer the question.

20. When offered something to drink (water, soda, coffee, tea), say yes. You'll probably need to wet your whistle from time to time.

21. Ask engineers about their responsibilities and what they like about the company.

22. Ask managers about the company, the products you'd be working on, and their "management style". Show interest in the product by asking intelligent questions about it.

23. Don't be afraid to ask for feedback from an interviewer at the end of a session.

24. Save questions about benefits for HR. Ofttimes you may touch base with the HR person again at the end of your interview day.

25. At this stage, a few companies may be ready to make you an offer. If so, skip down. If not, you will, we hope, get a phone call that goes something like this: "Hi, Sam. We really enjoyed talking with you the other day and would like to invite you back for a second interview. There are a couple more engineers who didn't get a chance to talk with you the first time we'd like you to meet the manager/director/vice president/president. When are you available to come in?"

26. The second interview may involve more engineers, but more often involves your boss's boss, their boss, and a longer session with HR. It is almost always less technical than the first, and is

more a formality to make sure the manager has the necessary approvals to extend an offer. Often, people's schedules dictate who will be there and who won't, and you might need to come back a third time to meet the company president.

27. When asked about salary, if you're a new graduate, just ask for "a competitive offer".

28. For someone more experienced, give a salary range if pressed for a number. Don't give a lower end that's lower than what you're willing to accept.

29. It's OK to answer the question, "What was your most recently salary?" But in general, defer questions about salary until it's clear that the company is seriously interested in you.

30. Always ask for stock options.

31. If by leaving your present position, you'd lose your vacation seniority, ask for the same number of vacation days per year to start.

32. It's especially good if you have an offer from another company. Don't reveal the name of the other company or the details of the offer; just the fact of its existence will strengthen your position.

You can talk about it in general, and how you'd weigh the comparative strengths and weaknesses of the offers, but it's a tricky negotiation.

33. When the company makes you an offer (yay.), it'll usually be within a week or so after your final interview. A formal offer letter will be sent by snail mail. It will have an expiration date a few days in the future. If you're sure, call the manager to accept. If not, reply with a counter-offer, but be sure it's one that's within the realm of possibility.

34. Most of all, good luck.

How to Lead a Team of Software Engineer

If your role includes leading a team of software engineers, then you'll need to refine your management and leadership skills. The main focus is on team cohesion and ensuring that each team member is achieving their best and has the necessary resources available to complete the tasks they've each been set.

Steps

1. Get the technical knowledge. Learn the software technologies you need to use in your project or product. Try to have good grasp on this knowledge, as you'll be teaching it to others and overseeing their efforts.

2. Get the domain knowledge. Try to learn the domain of product or project on which you are working. It facilitates better design of solution.

3. Be a good leader. Try to improve on your leadership. Be a good team leader.

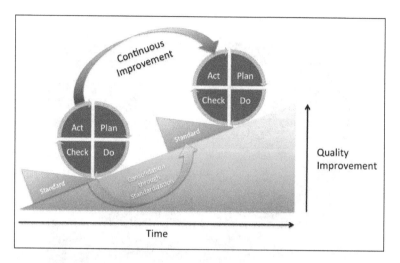

4. Have good management skills. Try to manage the work allocation efficiently.

5. Take responsibility. As a leader, take responsibility of not only for success but for failures too. Share the success and own the failure.

6. Have team spirit. As TEAM suggest "Together All Achieve More", embed it into your and your team's work life.

7. Build a good work culture. Work on building ethical, helpful and supportive team. It will lead to success for all.

CHAPTER 4

Software Testing

Software testing is the investigation of the quality of a product for determining its suitability for use and detecting software bugs, if any. This chapter explores some of the fundamental aspects of software testing and includes topics such as testing antivirus and security software, performing software product testing, categorizing software defects, using static analysis testing, etc.

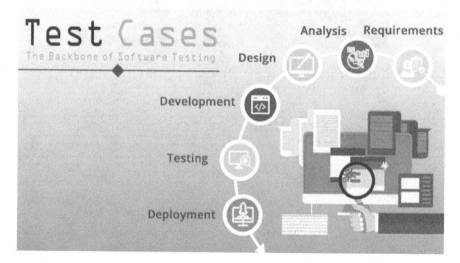

Software testing is an investigation conducted to provide stakeholders with information about the quality of the software product or service under test. Software testing can also provide an objective, independent view of the software to allow the business to appreciate and understand the risks of software implementation. Test techniques include the process of executing a program or application with the intent of finding software bugs (errors or other defects), and verifying that the software product is fit for use.

Software testing involves the execution of a software component or system component to evaluate one or more properties of interest. In general, these properties indicate the extent to which the component or system under test

- Meets the requirements that guided its design and development,

- Responds correctly to all kinds of inputs,

- Performs its functions within an acceptable time,

- Is sufficiently usable,

- Can be installed and run in its intended environments, and

- Achieves the general result its stakeholders desire.

As the number of possible tests for even simple software components is practically infinite, all software testing uses some strategy to select tests that are feasible for the available time and resources. As a result, software testing typically (but not exclusively) attempts to execute a program or application with the intent of finding software bugs (errors or other defects). The job of testing is an iterative process as when one bug is fixed, it can illuminate other, deeper bugs, or can even create new ones.

Software testing can provide objective, independent information about the quality of software and risk of its failure to users or sponsors.

Software testing can be conducted as soon as executable software (even if partially complete) exists. The overall approach to software development often determines when and how testing is conducted. For example, in a phased process, most testing occurs after system requirements have been defined and then implemented in testable programs. In contrast, under an agile approach, requirements, programming, and testing are often done concurrently.

Although testing can determine the correctness of software under the assumption of some specific hypotheses testing cannot identify all the defects within software. Instead, it furnishes a criticism or comparison that compares the state and behavior of the product against test oracles—principles or mechanisms by which someone might recognize a problem. These oracles may include (but are not limited to) specifications, contracts, comparable products, past versions of the same product, inferences about intended or expected purpose, user or customer expectations, relevant standards, applicable laws, or other criteria.

A primary purpose of testing is to detect software failures so that defects may be discovered and corrected. Testing cannot establish that a product functions properly under all conditions, but only that it does not function properly under specific conditions. The scope of software testing often includes examination of code as well as execution of that code in various environments and conditions as well as examining the aspects of code: does it do what it is supposed to do and do what it needs to do. In the current culture of software development, a testing organization may be separate from the development team. There are various roles for testing team members. Information derived from software testing may be used to correct the process by which software is developed.

Every software product has a target audience. For example, the audience for video game software is completely different from banking software. Therefore, when an organization develops or otherwise invests in a software product, it can assess whether the software product will be acceptable to its end users, its target audience, its purchasers and other stakeholders. Software testing aids the process of attempting to make this assessment.

Defects and Failures

Not all software defects are caused by coding errors. One common source of expensive defects is requirement gaps, e.g., unrecognized requirements that result in errors of omission by the program designer. Requirement gaps can often be non-functional requirements such as testability, scalability, maintainability, usability, performance, and security.

Software faults occur through the following processes. A programmer makes an error (mistake), which results in a defect (fault, bug) in the software source code. If this defect is executed, in certain situations the system will produce wrong results, causing a failure. Not all defects will necessarily result in failures. For example, defects in dead code will never result in failures. A defect can turn into a failure when the environment is changed. Examples of these changes in environment include the software being run on a new computer hardware platform, alterations in source data, or interacting with different software. A single defect may result in a wide range of failure symptoms.

Input Combinations and Preconditions

A fundamental problem with software testing is that testing under all combinations of inputs and preconditions (initial state) is not feasible, even with a simple product.:17–18 This means that the number of defects in a software product can be very large and defects that occur infrequently are difficult to find in testing. More significantly, non-functional dimensions of quality (how it is supposed to be versus what it is supposed to do)—usability, scalability, performance, compatibility, reliability—can be highly subjective; something that constitutes sufficient value to one person may be intolerable to another.

Software developers can't test everything, but they can use combinatorial test design to identify the minimum number of tests needed to get the coverage they want. Combinatorial test design enables users to get greater test coverage with fewer tests. Whether they are looking for speed or test depth, they can use combinatorial test design methods to build structured variation into their test cases.

Economics

A study conducted by NIST in 2002 reports that software bugs cost the U.S. economy $59.5 billion annually. More than a third of this cost could be avoided, if better software testing was performed.

Outsourcing software testing because of costs is very common, with China, the Philippines and India being preferred destinations.

Roles

Software testing can be done by dedicated software testers. Until the 1980s, the term "software tester" was used generally, but later it was also seen as a separate profession. Regarding the periods and the different goals in software testing, different roles have been established, such as test manager, test lead, test analyst, test designer, tester, automation developer, and test administrator. Software testing can also be performed by non-dedicated software testers.

Testing Process

Traditional Waterfall Development Model

A common practice in waterfall development is that testing is performed by an independent group of testers. This can happen:

- After the functionality is developed, but before it is shipped to the customer. This practice often results in the testing phase being used as a project buffer to compensate for project delays, thereby compromising the time devoted to testing.

- At the same moment the development project starts, as a continuous process until the project finishes.

However, even in the waterfall development model, unit testing is often done by the software development team even when further testing is done by a separate team.

Agile or XP Development Model

In contrast, some emerging software disciplines such as extreme programming and the agile software development movement, adhere to a "test-driven software development" model. In this process, unit tests are written first, by the software engineers (often with pair programming in the extreme programming methodology). The tests are expected to fail initially. Each failing test is followed by writing just enough code to make it pass. This means the test suites are continuously updated as new failure conditions and corner cases are discovered, and they are integrated with any regression tests that are developed. Unit tests are maintained along with the rest of the software source code and generally integrated into the build process (with inherently interactive tests being relegated to a partially manual build acceptance process).

The ultimate goals of this test process are to support continuous integration and to reduce defect rates.

This methodology increases the testing effort done by development, before reaching any formal testing team. In some other development models, most of the test execution occurs after the requirements have been defined and the coding process has been completed.

A Sample Testing Cycle

Although variations exist between organizations, there is a typical cycle for testing. The sample below is common among organizations employing the Waterfall development model. The same practices are commonly found in other development models, but might not be as clear or explicit.

- Requirements analysis: Testing should begin in the requirements phase of the software development life cycle. During the design phase, testers work to determine what aspects of a design are testable and with what parameters those tests work.

- Test planning: Test strategy, test plan, testbed creation. Since many activities will be carried out during testing, a plan is needed.

- Test development: Test procedures, test scenarios, test cases, test datasets, test scripts to use in testing software.

- Test execution: Testers execute the software based on the plans and test documents then report any errors found to the development team. This part could be complex when running tests with a lack of programming knowledge.

- Test reporting: Once testing is completed, testers generate metrics and make final reports on their test effort and whether or not the software tested is ready for release.

- Test result analysis: Or Defect Analysis, is done by the development team usually along with the client, in order to decide what defects should be assigned, fixed, rejected (i.e. found software working properly) or deferred to be dealt with later.

- Defect Retesting: Once a defect has been dealt with by the development team, it is retested by the testing team.

- Regression testing: It is common to have a small test program built of a subset of tests, for each integration of new, modified, or fixed software, in order to ensure that the latest delivery has not ruined anything and that the software product as a whole is still working correctly.

- Test Closure: Once the test meets the exit criteria, the activities such as capturing the key outputs, lessons learned, results, logs, documents related to the project are archived and used as a reference for future projects.

Automated Testing

Many programming groups[Like whom?] are relying more and more[vague] on automated testing, especially groups that use test-driven development. There are many frameworks[specify] to write tests in, and continuous integration software will run tests automatically every time code is checked into a version control system.

While automation cannot reproduce everything that a human can do (and all the ways they think of doing it), it can be very useful for regression testing. However, it does require a well-developed test suite of testing scripts in order to be truly useful.

Testing Tools

Program testing and fault detection can be aided significantly by testing tools and debuggers. Testing/debug tools include features such as:

- Program monitors, permitting full or partial monitoring of program code including:

  ○ Instruction set simulator, permitting complete instruction level monitoring and trace facilities

  ○ Hypervisor, permitting complete control of the execution of program code including:-

  ○ Program animation, permitting step-by-step execution and conditional breakpoint at source level or in machine code

  ○ Code coverage reports

- Formatted dump or symbolic debugging, tools allowing inspection of program variables on error or at chosen points

- Automated functional Graphical User Interface (GUI) testing tools are used to repeat system-level tests through the GUI

- Benchmarks, allowing run-time performance comparisons to be made

- Performance analysis (or profiling tools) that can help to highlight hot spots and resource usage.

Some of these features may be incorporated into a single composite tool or an Integrated Development Environment (IDE).

Measurement in Software Testing

Quality measures include such topics as correctness, completeness, security and ISO/IEC 9126 requirements such as capability, reliability, efficiency, portability, maintainability, compatibility, and usability.

There are a number of frequently used software metrics, or measures, which are used to assist in determining the state of the software or the adequacy of the testing.

Hierarchy of Testing Difficulty

Based on the amount of test cases required to construct a complete test suite in each context (i.e. a test suite such that, if it is applied to the implementation under test, then we collect enough information to precisely determine whether the system is correct or incorrect according to some specification), a hierarchy of testing difficulty has been proposed. It includes the following testability classes:

- Class I: there exists a finite complete test suite.

- Class II: any partial distinguishing rate (i.e., any incomplete capability to distinguish correct systems from incorrect systems) can be reached with a finite test suite.

- Class III: there exists a countable complete test suite.

- Class IV: there exists a complete test suite.

- Class V: all cases.

It has been proved that each class is strictly included in the next. For instance, testing when we assume that the behavior of the implementation under test can be denoted by a deterministic finite-state machine for some known finite sets of inputs and outputs and with some known number of states belongs to Class I (and all subsequent classes). However, if the number of states is not known, then it only belongs to all classes from Class II on. If the implementation under test must be a deterministic finite-state machine failing the specification for a single trace (and its continuations), and its number of states is unknown, then it only belongs to classes from Class III on. Testing temporal machines where transitions are triggered if inputs are produced within some real-bounded interval only belongs to classes from Class IV on, whereas testing many non-deterministic systems only belongs to Class V (but not all, and some even belong to Class I). The inclusion into Class I does not require the simplicity of the assumed computation model, as some testing cases involving implementations written in any programming language, and testing implementations defined as machines depending on continuous magnitudes, have been proved to be in Class I. Other elaborated cases, such as the testing framework by Matthew Hennessy under must semantics, and temporal machines with rational timeouts, belong to Class II.

Testing Artifacts

A software testing process can produce several artifacts. The actual artifacts produced are a factor of the software development model used, stakeholder and organisational needs.

Test Plan

A test plan is a document detailing the approach that will be taken for intended test activities. The plan may include aspects such as objectives, scope, processes and procedures, personnel requirements, and contingency plans. The test plan could come in the form of a single plan that includes all test types (like an acceptance or system test plan) and planning considerations, or it may be issued as a master test plan that provides an overview of more than one detailed test plan (a plan of a plan). A test plan can be, in some cases, part of a wide "test strategy" which documents overall testing approaches, which may itself be a master test plan or even a separate artifact.

Traceability Matrix

A traceability matrix is a table that correlates requirements or design documents to test documents. It is used to change tests when related source documents are changed, to select test cases for execution when planning for regression tests by considering requirement coverage.

Test Case

A test case normally consists of a unique identifier, requirement references from a design specification, preconditions, events, a series of steps (also known as actions) to follow, input, output, expected result, and the actual result. Clinically defined, a test case is an input and an expected result. This can be as terse as 'for condition x your derived result is y', although normally test cases describe in more detail the input scenario and what results might be expected. It can occasionally be a series of steps (but often steps are contained in a separate test procedure that can be exercised against multiple test cases, as a matter of economy) but with one expected result or expected outcome. The optional fields are a test case ID, test step, or order of execution number, related requirement(s), depth, test category, author, and check boxes for whether the test is automatable and has been automated. Larger test cases may also contain prerequisite states or steps, and descriptions. A test case should also contain a place for the actual result. These steps can be stored in a word processor document, spreadsheet, database, or other common repositories. In a database system, you may also be able to see past test results, who generated the results, and what system configuration was used to generate those results. These past results would usually be stored in a separate table.

Test Script

A test script is a procedure or programming code that replicates user actions. Initially, the term was derived from the product of work created by automated regression test tools. A test case will be a baseline to create test scripts using a tool or a program.

Test Suite

The most common term for a collection of test cases is a test suite. The test suite often also contains more detailed instructions or goals for each collection of test cases. It definitely contains a section where the tester identifies the system configuration used during testing. A group of test cases may also contain prerequisite states or steps, and descriptions of the following tests.

Test Fixture or Test Data

In most cases, multiple sets of values or data are used to test the same functionality of a particular feature. All the test values and changeable environmental components are collected in separate files and stored as test data. It is also useful to provide this data to the client and with the product or a project. There are techniques to generate test data.

Test Harness

The software, tools, samples of data input and output, and configurations are all referred to collectively as a test harness.

How to Test Software

Here are the essential software testing steps every software engineer should perform before showing their work to someone else.

1. Basic Functionality Testing

Begin by making sure that every button on every screen works. You also need to ensure that you can enter simple text into each field without crashing the software. You don't have to try out all the different combinations of clicks and characters, or edge conditions, because that's what your testers do—and they're really good at that. The goal here is this: don't let other people touch your work if it's going to crash as soon as they enter their own name into the username field. If the feature is designed to be accessed by way of an API, you need to run tests to make sure that the basic API functionality works before submitting it for more intensive testing. If your basic functionality testing detects something that doesn't work, that's fine. Just tell them that it doesn't work, that you're aware of it, and that they shouldn't bother trying it. You can fix it later, just don't leave any surprises in there.

2. Code Review

Another pair of eyes looking at the source code can uncover a lot of problems. If your coding methodology requires peer review, perform this step before you hand the code over for testing. Remember to do your basic functionality testing before the code review, though.

3. Static Code Analysis

There are tools that can perform analysis on source code or bytecode without executing it. These static code analysis tools can look for many weaknesses in the source code, such as security vulnerabilities and potential concurrency issues. Use static code analysis tools to enforce coding standards, and configure those tools to run automatically as part of the build.

4. Unit Testing

Developers will write unit tests to make sure that the unit (be it a method, class, or component) is working as expected and test across a range of valid and invalid inputs. In a continuous integration environment, unit tests should run every time you commit a change to the source code repository, and you should run them on your development machine as well. Some teams have coverage goals for their unit tests and will fail a build if the unit tests aren't extensive enough.

Developers also work with mock objects and virtualized services to make sure their units can be tested independently. If your unit tests fail, fix them before letting someone else use your code. If for any reason you can't fix them right now, let the other person know what has failed, so it won't come as a surprise when they come across the problem.

5. Single-user Performance Testing

Some teams have load and performance testing baked into their continuous integration process and run load tests as soon as code is checked in. This is particularly true for back-end code. But developers should also be looking at single-user performance on the front end and making sure the software is responsive when only they are using the system. If it's taking more than a few seconds to display a web page taken from a local or emulated (and therefore responsive) web server, find out what client-side code is slowing things down and fix it before you let someone else see it.

How to Test Antivirus and Security Software

Many antivirus utilities include protection against phishing, but some don't. Most suites include spam filtering, but some omit this feature, and some antivirus products add it as a bonus. Whatever features a given product offers, we put them to the test.

Testing Real-Time Antivirus

Every full-powered antivirus tool includes an on-demand scanner to seek out and destroy existing malware infestations and a real-time monitor to fend off new attacks. In the past, we've actually maintained a collection of malware-infested virtual machines to test each product's ability to remove existing malware. Advances in malware coding made testing with live malware too dangerous, but we can still exercise each product's real-time protection.

Each year in early spring, when most security vendors have finished their yearly update cycle, we gather a new collection of malware samples for this test. We start with a feed of the latest malware-hosting URLs, download hundreds of samples, and winnow them down to a manageable number.

We analyze each sample using various hand-coded tools. Some of the samples detect when they're running in a virtual machine and refrain from malicious activity; we simply don't use those. We look for a variety of different types, and for samples that make changes to the file system and Registry. With some effort, we pare the collection down to about 30, and record exactly what system changes each sample makes.

To test a product's malware-blocking abilities, we download a folder of samples from cloud storage. Real-time protection in some products kicks in immediately, wiping out known malware. If necessary to trigger real-time protection, we single-click each sample, or copy the collection to a new folder. We take note of how many samples the antivirus eliminates on sight.

Next, we launch each remaining sample and note whether the antivirus detected it. We record the total percentage detected, regardless of when detection happened.

Detection of a malware attack isn't sufficient; the antivirus must actually prevent the attack. A small in-house program checks the system to determine whether the malware managed to make any Registry changes or install any of its files. In the case of executable files, it also checks whether any of those processes are actually running. And as soon as measurement is complete, we shut down the virtual machine.

If a product prevents installation of all executable traces by a malware sample, it earns 8, 9, or 10 points, depending on how well it prevented cluttering the system with non-executable traces. Detecting malware but failing to prevent installation of executable components gets half-credit, 5 points. Finally, if, despite the antivirus's attempt at protection, one or more malware processes is actually running, that's worth a mere 3 points. The average of all these scores becomes the product's final malware-blocking score.

Testing Malicious URL Blocking

The best time to annihilate malware is before it ever reaches your computer. Many antivirus products integrate with your browsers and steer them away from known malware-hosting URLs. If protection doesn't kick in at that level, there's always an opportunity to wipe out the malware payload during or immediately after download.

While oue basic malware-blocking test uses the same set of samples for a season, the malware-hosting URLs we use to test Web-based protection are different every time. We get a feed of the very newest malicious URLs from London-based MRG-Effitas and typically use URLs that are no more than a day old.

Using a small purpose-built utility,we go down the list, launching each URL in turn. We discard any that don't actually point to a malware download, and any that return error messages. For the rest, we note whether the antivirus prevents access to the URL, wipes out the download, or does nothing. After recording the result, the utility jumps to the next URL in the list that isn't at the same domain. We do skip any files larger than 5MB, and also skip files that have already appeared in the same test. We keep at it until we've accumulated data for at least 100 verified malware-hosting URLs.

The score in this test is simply the percentage of URLs for which the antivirus prevented downloading malware, whether by cutting off access to the URL completely or by wiping out the downloaded file. Scores vary widely, but the very best security tools manage 90 percent or more.

Testing Phishing Detection

Why resort to elaborate data-stealing Trojans, when you can just trick people into giving up their passwords? That's the mindset of malefactors who create and manage phishing websites. These fraudulent sites mimic banks and other sensitive sites. If you enter your login credentials, you've just given away the keys to the kingdom. And phishing is platform-independent; it works on any operating system that supports browsing the Web.

These fake websites typically get blacklisted not long after their creation, so for testing we use only the very newest phishing URLs. We gather these from phishing-oriented websites, favoring those that have been reported as frauds but not yet verified. This forces security programs to use real-time analysis rather than relying on simple-minded blacklists.

Symantec's Norton Security has long been an outstanding detector of such frauds. Since the actual URLs used differ in every test, we report results as the difference between a product's detection rate and Norton's. We also compare the detection rate with that of the phishing protection built into Chrome, Firefox, and Internet Explorer.

We use five computers (most of them virtual machines) for this test, one protected by Norton, one by the product under testing, and one each using the three browsers alone. A small utility program launches each URL in the five browsers. If any of the five returns an error message, we discard that URL. If the resulting page doesn't actively attempt to imitate another site, or doesn't attempt to capture username and password data, we discard it. For the rest, we record whether or not each product detected the fraud.

In many cases, the product under testing can't even do as well as the built-in protection some browsers. Only a very few products come close to matching Norton's detection rate.

Testing Spam Filtering

These days email accounts for most consumers have the spam vacuumed out of them by the email provider, or by a utility running on the email server. In fact, the need for spam filtering is steadily dwindling. Austrian test lab AV-Comparatives tested antispam functionality a few years ago, finding that even Microsoft Outlook alone blocked almost 90 percent of spam, and most suites did better, some of them much better. The lab does not even promise to continue testing consumer-facing spam filters, noting that "several vendors are thinking of removing the antispam feature from their consumer security products."

In the past, we ran our own antispam tests using a real-world account that gets both spam and valid mail. The process of downloading thousands of messages and manually analyzing the contents of the Inbox and spam folder took more time and effort than any of the other hands-on tests. Expending maximal effort on a feature of minimal importance no longer makes sense.

There are still important points to report about a suite's spam filter. What email clients does it support? Can you use it with an unsupported client? Is it limited to POP3 email accounts, or does it also handle IMAP, Exchange, or even Web-based email? Going forward, we'll carefully consider each suite's antispam capabilities, but we will no longer be downloading and analyzing thousands of emails.

Testing Security Suite Performance

When your security suite is busily watching for malware attacks, defending against network intrusions, preventing your browser from visiting dangerous websites, and so on, it's clearly using some of your system's CPU and other resources to do its job. Some years ago, security suites got the reputation for sucking up so much of your system resources that your own computer use was affected. Things are a lot better these days, but we still run some simple tests to get an insight into each suite's effect on system performance.

Security software needs to load as early in the boot process as possible, lest it find malware already in control. But users don't want to wait around any longer than necessary to start using Windows after a reboot. Our test script runs immediately after boot and starts asking Windows to report the CPU usage level once per second. After 10 seconds in a row with CPU usage no more than 5 percent, it declares the system ready for use. Subtracting the start of the boot process (as reported by Windows) we know how long the boot process took. We run many repetitions of this test and compare the average with that of many repetitions when no suite was present.

In truth, you probably reboot no more than once per day. A security suite that slowed everyday file operations might have a more significant impact on your activities. To check for that kind of slowdown, we time a script that moves and copies a large collection of large-to-huge files between drives. Averaging several runs with no suite and several runs with the security suite active, we can determine just how much the suite slowed these file activities. A similar script measures the suite's effect on a script that zips and unzips the same file collection.

The average slowdown in these three tests by the suites with the very lightest touch can be as low as 1 percent. At the other end of the spectrum, a very few suites average 25 percent, or even more. You might actually notice the impact of the more heavy-handed suites.

Testing Firewall Protection

It's not as easy to quantify a firewall's success, because different vendors have different ideas about just what a firewall should do. Even so, there are a number of tests we can apply to most of them.

Typically a firewall has two jobs, protecting the computer from outside attack and ensuring that programs don't misuse the network connection. To test protection against attack, we use a physical computer that connects through the router's DMZ port. This gives the effect of a computer connected directly to the Internet. That's important for testing, because a computer that's connected through a router is effectively invisible to the Internet at large. We hit the test system with port scans and other Web-based tests. In most cases we find that the firewall completely hides the test system from these attacks, putting all ports in stealth mode.

The built-in Windows firewall handles stealthing all ports, so this test is just a baseline. But even here, there are different opinions. Kaspersky's designers don't see any value in stealthing ports as long as the ports are closed and the firewall actively prevents attack.

Program control in the earliest personal firewalls was extremely hands-on. Every time an unknown program tried to access the network, the firewall popped up a query asking the user whether or not to allow access. This approach isn't very effective, since the user generally has no idea what action is correct. Most will just allow everything. Others will click Block every time, until they break some important program; after that they allow everything. We perform a hands-on check of this functionality using a tiny browser utility coded in hour, one that will always qualify as an unknown program.

Some malicious programs attempt to get around this kind of simple program control by manipulating or masquerading as trusted programs. When we encounter an old-school firewall, we test its skills using utilities called leak tests. These programs use the same techniques to evade program control, but without any malicious payload. We do find fewer and fewer leak tests that still work under modern Windows versions.

At the other end of the spectrum, the best firewalls automatically configure network permissions for known good programs, eliminate known bad programs, and step up surveillance on unknowns. If an unknown program attempts a suspicious connection, the firewall kicks in at that point to stop it.

Software isn't and can't be perfect, so the bad guys work hard to find security holes in popular operating systems, browsers, and applications. They devise exploits to compromise system security using any vulnerabilities they find. Naturally the maker of the exploited product issues a security patch as soon as possible, but until you actually apply that patch, you're vulnerable.

The smartest firewalls intercept these exploit attacks at the network level, so they never even reach your computer. Even for those that don't scan at the network level, in many cases the antivirus component wipes out the exploit's malware payload. We use the CORE Impact penetration tool to hit each test system with about 30 recent exploits and record how well the security product fended them off.

Finally, we run a sanity check to see whether a malware coder could easily disable security protection. We look for an on/off switch in the Registry and test whether it can be used to turn off protection (though it's been years since we found a product vulnerable to this attack). We attempt to terminate security processes using Task Manager. And we check whether it's possible to stop or disable the product's essential Windows services.

Testing Parental Control

Parental control and monitoring covers a wide variety of programs and features. The typical parental control utility keeps kids away from unsavory sites, monitors their Internet usage, and lets parents determine when and for how long the kids are allowed to use the Internet each day. Other features range from limiting chat contacts to patrolling Facebook posts for risky topics.

we always perform a sanity check to make sure the content filter actually works. As it turns out, finding porn sites for testing is a snap. Just about any URL composed of a size adjective and the name of a normally-covered body part is already a porn site. Very few products fail this test.

We use a tiny in-house browser utility to verify that content filtering is browser independent. We issue a three-word network command (no, I'm not publishing it here) that disables some simple-minded content filters. And we check whether we can evade the filter by using a secure anonymizing proxy website.

Imposing time limits on the children's computer or Internet use is only effective if the kids can't interfere with timekeeping. We verify that the time-scheduling feature works, then try evading it by resetting the system date and time. The best products don't rely on the system clock for their date and time.

After that, it's simply a matter of testing the features that the program claims to have. If it promises the ability to block use of specific programs, we engage that feature and try to break it by moving, copying, or renaming the program. If it says it strips out bad words from email or instant messaging, we add a random word to the block list and verify that it doesn't get sent. If it claims it can limit instant messaging contacts, we set up a conversation between two of our accounts and then ban one of them. Whatever control or monitoring power the program promises, we do our best to put it to the test.

How to Perform Software Product Testing

Software Products need their own unique approach to test adequately and correctly. Often times, teams treat them as any other software (i.e. internal applications built for a specific client or team; not accessible by the general public; non-revenue generating) and that is the starting point of trouble.

Software Product Testing needs a custom test style and strategy to add value. Software Product development and sustenance is in itself a complex ecosystem and to thrive testers need to adapt.

This is product test process, method, or life-cycle at each stage.

Stage 1. Product Introduction

Since this is the first time TrackFast would be going out into the market, the idea is to make a good first impression. So leave no stone unturned. Test everything and from every angle. In addition to that, lay the foundation for future testing.

A good test strategy at this point should include the following:

- Tests that validate the short term goals of TrackFast. "What does it need to be shipped correctly" should be at the forefront of the testing effort. Create End to end tests (front end, middleware, and backend) for thorough testing of every feature

- Tests that compare TrackFast with the competition (ideally this is the job of product owners but as a tester we can add our two cents. Also, this step is easier if the software has some peers already. For example: It is easy to compare TrackFast with Bugzilla or JIRA or other legacy systems. But let us say I am creating an app that does something unusual like being able to predict when a baby is hungry or cranky :), it might be hard to find an application that you can use as a baseline)

- Platform, browser and device compatibility tests

- Tests for ease of installation, set up and getting-up-to-speed

- Tests for performance, security, and usability

- Integration Tests if it interfaces with other systems. A simple integration example is that Defect tracking systems often interact with email clients to send notifications

- Plan for regression– It is a good idea to flag or mark critical tests that you think will be a part of future regression cycles and think about automating them for future releases

- Plan for known issues (are you going to be adding them to the backlog or handling them as CRs, etc.)

- Flexibility to change when the product progresses to the next life cycle stage.

It could sometimes be a long wait before the product goes out, so use all the time you have to do as thorough a job as possible.

In this stage, though there is a piece of the product ready at the end of 2-4 week sprints, most often every sprint does not result in shipped code. Therefore, never consider last sprint testing 'done-and-delivered'. Repeat critical tests with every sprint until release. With each sprint, test the entire product that you have until that point.

Stage 2. Product Growth

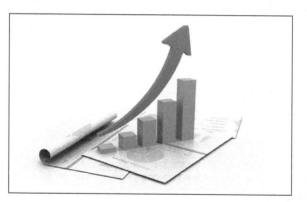

After the initial project introduction, if all goes well, expect an influx of activity because Product Growth is a fast paced lane. You are now swimming along with the big sharks and unless you keep up, you get gobbled down.

Here, the releases get shorter, the improvements done to the software become more in number and extent of regression almost becomes unmanageable.

The product testing strategy should work with the pace that the software development is proceeding and should not become a bottleneck.

These can help:

- Keep in mind the long-term goals of the project. It is not about getting-it-over-with now. It is about living with the features and thriving with them.

- Test Early- Consider TDD or BDD instead of deferring testing to the end with new requirements

- Automate Regression and strengthen it– Create an automated regression suite in place so you are not left with untested landmines in your system

- If your business/product owners want to get involved with testing, consider a business language based automation tool such as Cucumber.

- Keep usability and site design central to your testing. Because the more features we add, the cleaner the site should look

- Perform performance and security testing when a major release has happened or there is a significant change made to the architecture. (New server brought in, etc.) Most software systems don't need this with every release.

- Keep in touch with the competition and know the product vision

- Adapt pair testing, for immediate feedback and fixing. Include the product owner when possible

- Plan for changes and known issues

- Try to get your hands on the customer feedback and check if they are can be tracked as enhancement suggestion to keep the growth constant. (once again, this is not the primary responsibility of the QA team, but everyone counts)

Stage 3. Product Maturity

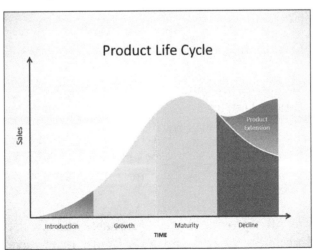

Congratulations that your product has come this far. At this point, the features don't change as often. The product team is going to be more focused on bringing more business or their marketing efforts. However, product development and testing need not and often don't stop.

Therefore, the testing team can:

- Work on maturing your test strategy. By this point, your regression suites, test design methods, and test management practices must work like well-oiled machines.

- Focus on the finer details. Because overall the product works and is doing well, but as they say- 'God is in the details'– find even the smallest of the problems that can improve the quality of the system

- Consider customer feedback

- Test Performance and security periodically

- Take into account the new devices, platforms, and browsers that might have come into the market from the last time you tested

- Test User Manual and FAQ pages because by now you have the time and you can afford to.

- Experiment with a new product test tools, services or a process because now you can.

- Test the installation process with every release, however small that might be and get statistics as to how easy or difficult it is for the end user.

Whatever you do, don't get complacent.

Stage 4. Product Decline/Circling back to Product Growth

The product owners and businesses are smart these days and know very well that they can't keep their product the same and expect the users to stay loyal. Things move too fast and so do products.

So, TrackFast can't sit back and relax. If it needs to have a continued market presence and stay the leader, it needs to evolve. Like it or hate it, Facebook started as a simple social network to connect people and it is a large software platform in itself integrating with a million other things and staying current.

TrackFast too has to evolve. After proving that it is a reliable and effective defect tracking system, it has to evolve or it will decline. So, the company XYZ decides to improve TrackFast by making it a general ticketing system that can be used to track any incidents or cases by the business other than IT/test teams (something like JIRA) and not just for defects in the software development process.

The wheel has made a full turn and you find yourself treating the system as a brand new one and follow the strategy. Only now you are more experienced and familiar with the drill. But remember, with each new turn comes a new challenge. So stay sharp.

How to Install an SSD in a Netbook and Test the Speed Improvement with HD Tune

An SSD (Solid State Drive) is a computer HDD (hard drive disk) based on flash memory technology. It works under the same principles as your good old USB key.

A HDD has 3 speed ratings: read, write and seek. The main components we are looking for when improving speed performance is the seek time, but most importantly, the read time. The faster a HDD can read files, the faster the computer can display it. An SSD can be up to 5 times faster than an ordinary HDD. As a bonus, SSDs are much lighter and require less power than ordinary HDDs thus making your netbook lighter and your battery last longer.

Steps

1. Take your stopwatch and start it at the same time you turn on your netbook. When your operating system loads (Windows or Linux), double click to open an internet window. Stop the stopwatch when the internet window is showing your home page. Note the time it took. This is your load time. (The time can be a rough estimation if you want, i.e. : 1 min or 50 s.)

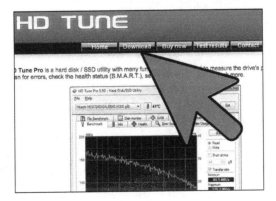

2. Visit HD Tune and download the latest version.

3. Open and run the program. Start the test in the "Benchmark" tab. The running time may take up to 5 minutes depending on your hard drive speed. Once the program is done note the seek time and average transfer rate.

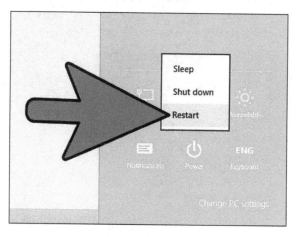

4. Shut down the computer and remove the battery.

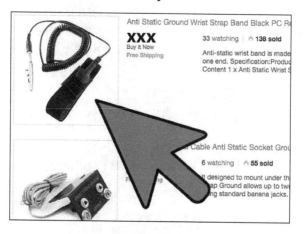

5. Make sure you ground yourself before touching the internal parts of the netbook. To do so, simply touch the screw on a wall outlet. This will remove all static electricity built up in your body that could damage the fragile computer parts.

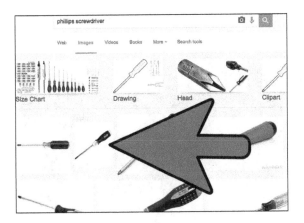

6. Take your Philips screwdriver and open the back cover of the netbook to expose the HDD and RAM. If there is more than one cover you can open, the one for the HDD is marked with 2 arrows pointing towards a circle in the middle. A little force may be required, sometimes a lot, be careful not to snap anything.

7. Remove all the necessary screws to free ONLY the HDD. (If you are not sure you can take it apart and put it back together it is suggested you take a picture before every step you do so you will have a visual aid to re-do what you did backwards.) Sometimes a metal encasing can be holding the HDD, like in my case, make sure to remove it also.

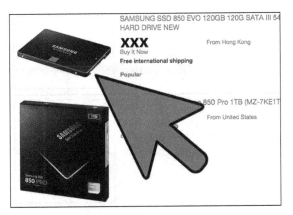

8. Switch the old HDD with the new SSD. Re-assemble everything. Make sure not to forget any screws or not to tight them too much. (If the metal starts bending, it might be a sign that it is too tight.)

9. Plug in the AC adapter for your netbook and plug in the external DVD reader. Insert your Operating system DVD.

10. Turn on the computer and press F2 or DEL when the manufacturer logo screen appears to access your computer's BIOS. By default the computer is looking at the HDD for instructions on what to do but since your HDD is empty, we need to tell it to look at the DVD instead. Once in the BIOS, look for an option called Booting, Boot sequence, Boot, Startup or something similar. Make sure the DVD reader is selected as your primary boot device. Exit and save BIOS.

Install your Operating System

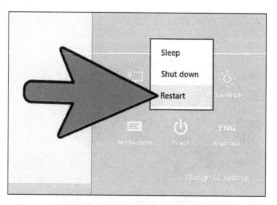

1. Re-start the computer, access your BIOS again and make sure to put your now formatted SSD as your first boot device. Exit and save BIOS. Unplug DVD reader, you are done with it.

2. Re-start computer and time the load time like before.

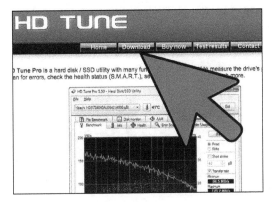

3. Download and run HD Tune. Once again, your numbers will be much faster.

How to Find a Bug by Isolating

This method is a very useful method for finding a bug, when it is hard to find, especially on HTML and XML (because there aren't debuggers or break points).

Steps

1. Make a backup of your source. You will want a checkpoint that you can go back because you will go back later.

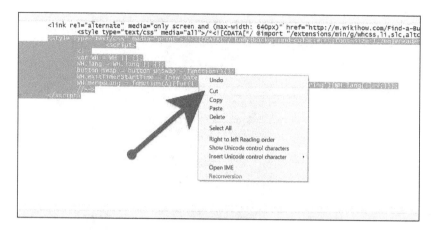

2. Erase a small section, and put in the small something instead. Like a message box, a white space, a constant number variable (to erase an algorithm), etc. Sometimes, the placeholder will have to have the same size as the part you took out. You can do anything to it, because you have the backup.

3. See the result. Does it work perfectly now? The bug was in the erased part, so go to the next step. Does it work even funkier than before? Undo the erased part and try again. Does it give the same results as last time? At least you know it isn't there.

4. Go smaller. Undo the erased part, put markers around it, and try to find the exact place of the bug by the same method, in the markers.

How to make Test Automation Effective in an Agile Environment

Today, more and more software development companies are shifting to an agile development approach from traditional waterfall development to keep pace with the current trends.To meet the demands of agile environment, several companies have adopted test automation which resolves some of the issues faced in manual testing and delivers faster results.

Even though test automation provides assistance in many ways, there are several challenges in test automation which can turn out to be a nightmare if it is adopted without appropriate brainstorming and analysis. Here's a complete guide to make test automation work successfully in agile environment.

Steps

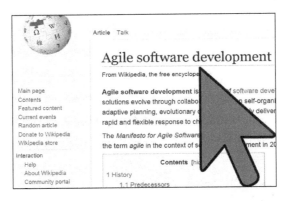

1. Allocate enough timings. Since in agile development there is a continuous release of various iterations, the team usually misses out on the quality. Even worse, when there are several sprints which require fixing, it becomes really tough for the team to devote time in developing, fixing and testing each iteration.

- It is necessary for the team to allocate enough time for testing. It is advisable to start test automation parallel to development so that there are no lags. This will help the team in becoming more productive and respond to the results quickly and avoid last minute rushes. Moreover, it will also help testers to devote time in exploratory test which requires manual efforts.

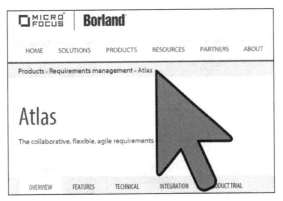

2. Developing quality test scripts keeping in mind regression testing needs. Teams should develop quality test scripts keeping in mind the regression testing concept. Developing quality test scripts

here means, ensuring that the test scripts meet the below mentioned criteria: correctness, maintainability, versioning, integrity, portability, performance.

- The objective behind this is to run testing especially regression testing smoothly and correctly without any intervention from the testers. If the test scripts are developed in the regression testing concept, the team would be able to complete the testing without much changes in the scripts and can also avail the benefits of performance, speed and accuracy.

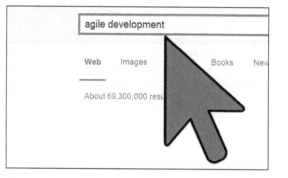

3. Get the right automation tool. Testing team should also understand the fact that if it's not the right automation tool, nothing's going to be right. A lot of effort should be involved while evaluating and purchasing a test automation tool. One should always refer to the criteria or requirements before selecting a test automation. Below are some of the features/criteria that an ideal test automation tool should have/meet

- The test automation tool you choose should be OS friendly. Larger the number of operating systems it supports, better it becomes for teams to perform testing

- Test automation tool should also be in line with your budget and should incorporate features in terms of its pricing and licensing

- The tool should have easy to understand architecture. Meaning, the UI, navigation and functionality should be user-friendly so that even a layman can operate it. There are certain testing tools with codeless architecture which means, testers need not write codes and can test the applications in minutes

- The automation tool you choose should be able to give quick results and reporting abilities so that testers can quickly respond to the requirements of the agile testing environment

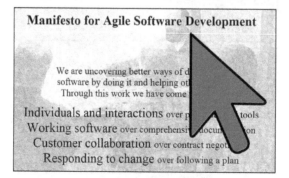

4. Keep a bird's eye on development environment. The teams should understand and check their development environment which consists of simple virtual machines to cloud environments that

deals with external services and database. Any bug or problem in the application may be the result of network problems, configurations, unavailability of services, backend data, etc. Without good understanding or monitoring of the actual environment, teams would be juggling with the root causes and would waste their time instead of achieving the results. Hence it is imperative to get complete knowledge about the development environment and their aspects before implementing test automation so that teams can divert their attention in improving the quality and not in finding the causes of defects.

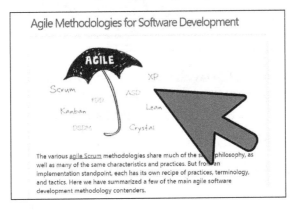

5. Keep your tests small and lean. Keeping tests cases small and lean really helps avoid the unnecessary test data that do not require testing or add no value to the actual result. It also helps in dealing with complex scenarios since the test cases are small. Moreover, teams do not require analyzing large suite of test cases which contain different codes, scenarios, configurations etc. Smaller and incremental test cases also reduces the load on the agile development environment and helps in evaluating the cost vs. ROI figure for every lot.

How to Run Jmeter Scripts on Remote Servers

Where to place .csv files, what properties to edit, and how to run jmeter scripts on remote servers. Knowledge of running jmeter scripts locally is required. Example setup involves one client and 5 remote servers all on the same local network.

Steps

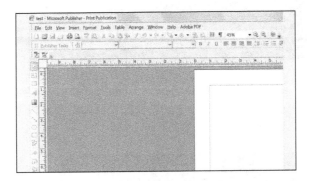

1. Divide .csv file into multiple files. (Example: If your .csv file contains 500 entries and you're using 5 remote servers, divide your .csv file into 5 files containing 100 entries each). Place the .csv files in the jmeter/bin/ directory of each remote server.

2. Open 'jmeter' (located in jmeter/bin) with a text editor. Edit Heap values to higher values based on available ram. (ex: if you have 15GB ram on a server, try heap values of 12,288 and 13,312, this leaves a little free for other processes.) Do this on client and remote servers.

3. Open 'jmeter.properties' (located in jmeter/bin) with a text editor. On servers, remove the # in front of hold. This mode requires more memory but helps prevent your test data from being corrupted by the constant streaming of data to the client (hold mode waits until the test is finished before sending data back to client). On client, find the line 'remote_hosts=127.0.0.1'. Replace 127.0.0.1 with the internal IP addresses of your remote servers. (ex: remote_hos ts=10.1.1.144,10.1.1.35,10.1.1.56,10.1.1.34,10.1.1.140)

4. Launch jmeter-server from a command prompt on each server. Launch your jmeter script from the client using 'remote start all'.

How to Improve Software Testing

The best practices for improving software testing and for increasing the quality of your software products.

1. Plan the testing and QA processes

Test processes should be well planned, defined, and documented. Good documentation is the tool that builds efficient communication within the software team. So, effective planning entails the creation of the quality and test plans for a project.

QUALITY ASSURANCE PLANNING				
Hierarchy	Goals	Review policy	Key elements	Users
Quality management plan				
Product	Define quality standards and quality assurance objectives	Rarely reviewed	✓ Quality objectives ✓ Key deliverables ✓ Quality standards ✓ Roles ✓ Tools	Stakeholders, QA specialists, developers
Test plan				
Product version, feature set, environment	Cover test scope and activities for product version, feature set, etc.	Regularly reviewed	✓ Test items ✓ Test approach ✓ Pass and fail criteria ✓ Features to be tested ✓ Deliverables ✓ Schedule ✓ Risks ✓ Assumptions	QA specialists, developers
Test case				
Feature	Define testing conditions to verify the expected functionality of a feature	Constantly reviewed	✓ Test case ID ✓ Description ✓ Test steps ✓ Data ✓ Expected result ✓ Actual result ✓ Date of creation ✓ Status	QA specialists developers

Quality Management Plan

A quality management plan is a document that defines an acceptable level of product quality and describes how the project will achieve this level. It isn't a mandatory document, but it will help you schedule all the tasks needed to make sure that the project meets your customer's needs and expectations. The main goal of this plan is to support project managers. Accordingly, it should include the software's quality requirements and describe how they should be assessed.

Key components of the quality management plan:

- Quality objectives
- Key project deliverables and processes to be reviewed for satisfactory quality level
- Quality standards
- Quality control and assurance activities
- Quality roles and responsibilities
- Quality tools
- Plan for reporting quality control and assurance problems

Test Plan

A test plan is a document that describes what to test, when to test, how to test, and who will do the tests. It also describes the testing scope and activities. The test plan includes the objectives of the tests to be run and helps control the risks. It's a good practice to have a test plan written by an experienced person like a QA lead or manager. The test plan must be a guidebook for the testing process and it should cover:

- The scope of testing
- Test objectives
- Budget limitations
- Deadlines
- Test execution schedule
- Risks identifications

A good test plan should include the schedule for all necessary testing activities in order to control your team testing time. It also should define the roles of every team member so that everyone is clear about what is required of them. There's no universal way of creating a test plan because it depends on the processes, standards, and test management tools implemented in the company. A test plan document should contain the following information:

- Test plan identifier
- Introduction
- References (list of related documents)
- Test items (the product and its versions)
- Features to be tested
- Features not to be tested
- Item pass or fail criteria
- Test approach (testing levels, types, techniques)
- Suspension criteria
- Deliverables (Test Plan, the document itself, Test Cases, Test Scripts, Defect/Enhancement Logs, Test Reports
- Test environment (hardware, software, tools)
- Estimates
- Schedule
- Staffing and training needs
- Responsibilities

- Risks

- Assumptions and Dependencies

- Approvals

Here are some key guidelines for making the test plan more effective:

Make your test plan brief. Avoid repetition or irrelevance. It should contain only the relevant information.

Be specific. Include all details, e.g. editions and versions of the programs, to make the document searchable

Update a test plan. It's a live document that must be frequently updated on an on-demand basis.

Share a test plan with your stakeholders. It will give them information about your testing processes. The quality of your test plan will represent the quality of the testing your team will to perform.

Test Cases

Preparation of effective test cases is an integral part of software testing improvements. According to the definition, given by ISTQB (International Software Testing Qualifications Board, the worldwide leader in the certification of competences in software testing) "a test case is a document which consists of a set of conditions or actions which are performed on the software application in order to verify the expected functionality of the feature". It's one of the key instruments used by testers. The standard test case includes the following information:

- The test case ID

- Test case description

- Prerequisites

- Test steps

- Test data

- Expected result

- Actual result

- Status

- Created by

- Date of creation

- Executed by

- Date of execution

Below you can see the example of a standard test case.

Test case ID	Test case description	Prerequisites	Test steps	Test data	Expected Result	Actual Result	Status	Created By	Date of creation	Executed By	Date of execution
TC001	The objective of this test case is to verify the 'Login' of Gmail account	1. User is authorized 2. Has an account in Gmail	1. Enter valid username 2. Enter valid password 3. Click on 'Login' button	1. User account should be present in Gmail	1. User should be able to login his Gmail account with his valid credentials 2. 'Invalid username or password' should get displayed if the username and password are not valid	1. If the valid credentials are entered then the user will be able to login his / her account 2. If invalid credentials are entered then nothing happens(the expected message is not displayed)	Fail	Rajesh	1/1/2016	Umesh	1/2/2016

Use the following practices to write effective test cases :

Identify testable requirements. Identify the scope and purpose of testing before starting the test process.

Customer requirement. The specialist who writes the test case must have a good understanding of the features and user requirements. Each test case should be written keeping the client's requirements in mind.

Write on time. The best time to write test cases is the early requirement analysis and design phases. That way QA specialists can understand whether all requirements are testable or not.

Simple and clear. Test cases should be simple and easy to understand. Every test case should include only the necessary and relevant steps. No matter how many times and by whom it will be used, a test case must have a single expected result rather than multiple expected results.

Unique test cases. Each test case must have a unique name. This will help classify, track, and review test cases at later stages.

Test cases should be maintainable. If requirements change, a tester must be able to maintain a test case.

2. Employ Test-oriented Software Development Management

Implementation of test-oriented management approaches is a good way to improve the quality of software. One of the ways to achieve this is using extreme programming (EX) – a software development methodology that aims to produce higher quality software with the ability to adapt to changing requirements. Let's take a closer look at the following extreme programming practices:

- Test-driven development
- Pair programming

Test-driven Development

Test-driven development (TDD) is a software development process in which tests are written before any implementation of code. TDD has a test-first approach based on repetition of a very short development cycle. According to it, each new feature begins with writing a test. The developer writes an automated test case before he/she writes enough production code to fulfill that test. This test case will initially fail. The next step will be to write the code focusing on functionality to get that test passed. After these steps are completed, a developer refactors the code to pass all the tests.

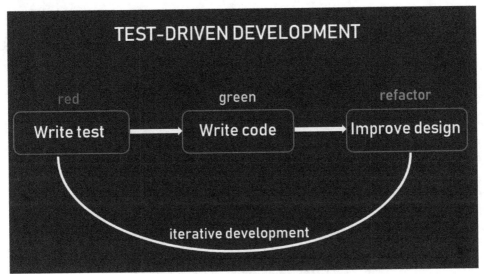

Test-Driven Development lifecycle

The following are the benefits of using the TDD approach:

- High quality. The quality of TDD-based products is usually much higher than that achieved with other methods.

- Optimization of development costs. The cost of debugging at later stages is minimized as tests are run from the beginning of the design cycle.

- Simplification of code. Engineers invest more effort in aligning code requirements to particular tests.

- Positive effects on productivity. The TDD approach provides quick feedback on introducing a bug and fixing it. A developer notices a bug as soon as the test fails and then fixes it to pass the test again.

Executable documentation. Use-cases are written as tests and other developers can view the tests as examples of how the code is supposed to work.

Pair Programming

Pair programming is also an extreme programming technique. This development approach requires two engineers working in tandem at a single computer. One of them writes a code while the other watches and makes suggestions through the process. These roles can be swapped at any time. Two developers working at a single computer will produce software with a significantly higher quality. The increased code quality can reduce the debugging and refactoring cost of the project in the long run.

The benefits of pair programming:

- High code quality. Fewer mistakes and bugs are introduced into the code as problems are caught before or during the code writing.

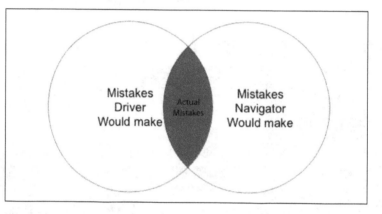

- Better knowledge sharing among team members. You will have more people who know how the product works. In this case, if one of the pair leaves the company, there will be someone remaining who is experienced with the code.

- Clear code. You will receive shorter and much clearer code.

- Two heads are better than one. If some problems crop up along the way, two people can solve them faster than one.

3. Ensure Suitable Work Environment for QA Team

Involve the dedicated QA team from the beginning to start testing early

Testing should be done by a dedicated team. In this case, you will be assured that testing is done professionally. Making quality improvements must be part of the team members goals. Testers must be involved in the software design process from the start. It helps ensure that they will be able to solve any problems that arise before the cost of resolving an issue starts growing exponentially.

Respect your Testers

If you want to achieve high-level quality goals, you need to build trusting relationships between a QA team and developers with respect for each other. Also, it would be better to search for people with coding skills. Obviously, engineers will respect such testers more. They will also be able to code some of their own testing tools. Such an approach provides for better communication between both sides, testers, and developers. A QA lead has to recognize the progress of the team and individual achievements of its members at team meetings. It will encourage other specialists to do better work in the future.

Give Business Training to your QA Team

Provide the necessary pieces of training for your QA specialists to expand their knowledge. You can organize training sessions and other team building exercises to improve the work of the entire team. A QA team lead should organize brainstorming sessions to create the floods of collective creativity in the team. It will help invent new techniques for solving existing problem.

Importance of Communication

Collocate your testers and developers to improve communication efficiency. Face-to-face communication will help avoid misunderstandings. Good communication within the team allows people to compare results and share effective solutions to problems encountered during tests. You also need a good team leader who will be able to effectively share feedback and ideas with testers. QA managers should encourage team members to speak about existing problems and other issues with the team that could impact productivity and efficiency.

It's also important to give your testers a chance to talk about things privately, separately from group meetings. QA leaders should be flexible and open to new strategies to best serve their teams.

4. Optimize the use of Automated tests

If you really want to improve the quality of your software, then automated testing is definitely worth taking into consideration. Two of three key trends are increasing test automation and widespread adoption of the Agile methodologies. It's really a wise recommendation to deploy automated testing throughout the QA process. Automated testing means using automation tools to run the tests.

While automated testing can be employed within traditional Agile workflows, it can also be a part of a broader practice called continuous integration.

Continuous Integration and Continuous Delivery

Continuous delivery is considered an evolutionary development of the Agile principles. This method means that you can release changes to your customers quickly in a sustainable way. CD allows the commitment of new pieces of code when they are ready without short release iterations. Generally, you automatically deploy every change that passes the tests. This is achieved by a high level of testing and deployment automation.

Continuous integration describes how the continuous delivery method is implemented at the software engineering level. It's a development practice that requires engineers to integrate the changes into a product several times a day. Each code piece runs the "integration tests" at every code change to detect errors and bugs quickly, and locate them more easily. A good practice is to combine the CI with the automated testing to make your code dependable. Bamboo, Hudson, and Cruise Control are open source tools that allow for introduction of continuous integration in your environment.

How to use Static Analysis Testing

Step 1. Finalize the Tool

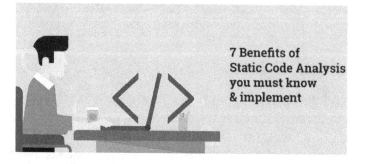

7 Benefits of
Static Code Analysis
you must know
& implement

The first step is to finalize the tool capable of performing static analysis of the different applications in your firm. The tools need to understand not only the programming languages used, but also the underlying/dependent frameworks used by the software. Some additional factors to consider include IDE support, cost of the tool, and infrastructure requirements for the tool. This might involve detailed analysis of the different static analysis tools available to determine which tools best satisfy your needs.

In cases where tools do not adequately support the languages or frameworks being used, manual code reviews can be performed as a supplemental activity.

Step 2. Create a Scanning Infrastructure and Deploy the Tool

Now that you have decided on the tool to use, create an infrastructure to deploy the tool. This might involve handling licensing requirements of the tool, access control and authorization to access the tool, and procuring the resources required (e.g. servers and databases) to deploy.

Step 3. Customize the Tool

Once the tool is deployed and in use among the different teams, it's time to customize the tool to further suit your needs. This could include integrating the scanning tools to build environments, creating dashboards for tracking scan results, and building custom reporting.

```
/**
 * Returns a {@link java.util.concurrent.Callable} which can be used to resolve the {@link HarvestOp}
 * related to this {@link Task}.
 * <p>
 * If you attempt to resolve the {@link java.util.concurrent.Callable} returned by this method
 * inside the {@link UnprocessedTask} it will cause a {@link StackOverflowError} due to an
 * infinite loop between the {@code Task} trying to resolve the {@link HarvestOp} and the
 * {@link HarvestOp} trying to resolve the task. This is why an {@link Association} is passed to
 * the final {@link Task} object and resolved at a later time after construction has completed.
 *
 * @return The callable to resolve the harvest op.
 */
@CarefulNow
public HttpCallable<HarvestOp> getHarvestOp() {
    return new GetHarvestOpsByIdCallable(mForestHqSession, mRawSimpleTask.operation_id);
}
```

The tools can also be tuned to reduce false positives or find additional vulnerabilities in frameworks used by development teams.

Step 4. Prioritize and On-board

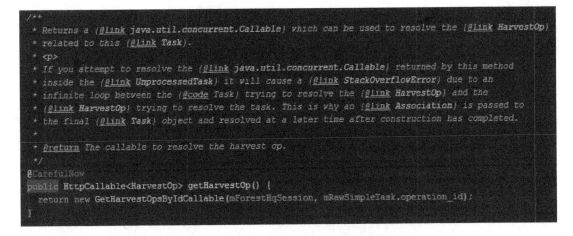

Many enterprises have a large number of applications that can be put through the scanning program. Your firm can prioritize these applications to ensure that the highest-risk applications are scanned first. As time progresses, the majority of the applications can be on-boarded to the scanning infrastructure. The code to be analyzed with a tool needs to be compilable and include all the libraries used within, or in association with, the software.

Once on-boarded with the tool, the applications should be scanned regularly. This can take place by syncing application scans to the release cycle, daily or monthly builds, or every time the code is checked in.

Step 5. Analyze Results

After the applications are scanned, a security analyst must assess and triage results for false positives. Discovered vulnerabilities should be tracked and provided to the development teams in order to conduct remediation in a timely manner.

Step 6. Governance and Training

A governance program is required to ensure that different teams utilize the scanning tools correctly. The software security touchpoints should be present within the software development life cycle (SDLC). SAST should be incorporated as part of the application development and deployment process.

The scanning results should be tracked to ensure that the critical or high priority issues identified by the tools are fixed before the application is deployed into production. Additionally, you can create language and framework-specific secure coding and remediation guidelines for common security vulnerabilities. This can be used as a resource for developers to refer to during the development phase, as well as for fixing vulnerabilities discovered by the tool.

How to Categorize Software Defects

Computer programming defects are categorized in order to emphasize the severity of the defects discovered during testing. In many software companies, this process is known as "bug triage" and is done on a regular basis near the end of the development life cycle. It often involves the collaborative efforts of project manager, development manager, QA managers, and other technical staff.

There are altogether six defect categories, which help the software developers to prioritize their tasks. That means this kind of grading help the developers in fixing those defects first that are highly crucial.

Steps

1. Categorize as 'Show Stopper' if the defects detected are so severe that it has to be fixed before the tester can continue with testing.

2. Categorize as 'Critical' those defects that need to be fixed before the application can be released into production. But these defects do not hamper the continuation of the testing process.

3. Categorize as 'Major' those defects that do not obstruct the continuance of the testing process but will cause great deviation from the business requirements if released for production.

4. Use the classification of 'Medium' for those defects that do not hinder the continuation of the testing process and which result in only minimal deviation from the business requirements when in production.

5. Assign the status of 'Minor' to those Defects that do not affect the continuance of the testing process and which show little or no deviation from the business requirements.

6. Call them 'Cosmetic' if the defects are negligible and inconsequential unless and until it doesn't show a great deviation from business requirements. For instance, issues like fonts, colors or pitch size affect neither the continuation of the testing process nor the application's release into production.

Software Maintenance

Software maintenance refers to the process by which a software product is modified and refined to correct faults and improve performance. The topics elucidated in this chapter address some of the techniques of software maintenance such as for improving software quality, fixing bugs, managing a new software implementation, finding XPath using Firebug, etc.

Software maintenance in software engineering is the modification of a software product after delivery to correct faults, to improve performance or other attributes. The key software maintenance issues are both managerial and technical. Key management issues are alignment with customer priorities, staffing, which organisation does maintenance, estimating costs. Key technical issues are: limited understanding, impact analysis, testing, maintainability measurement. Software Maintenance Processes Following are some of the software maintenance processes

- The implementation process contains software preparation and transition activities, such as the conception and creation of the maintenance plan, the preparation for handling problems identified during development, and the follow-up on product configuration management.

- The problem and modification analysis process, which is executed once the application has become the responsibility of the maintenance group. The maintenance programmer must analyse each request, confirm it (by reproducing the situation) and check its validity, investigate it and propose a solution, document the request and the solution proposal, and finally, obtain all the required authorisations to apply the modifications.

- The process considering the implementation of the modification itself.

- The process acceptance of the modification, by confirming the modified work with the individual who submitted the request in order to make sure the modification provided a solution.

- The migration process (platform migration, e.g., is exceptional, and is not part of daily maintenance tasks. If the software must be ported to another platform without any change in functionality, this process will be used and a maintenance project team is likely to be assigned to this task.

- Finally, the last maintenance process, also an event which does not occur on a daily basis, is the retirement of a piece of software.

Software Change

There are four categories of software change:

- Corrective
- Adaptive
- Perfective
- Preventive

Corrective Change

Corrective change, most commonly referred to as "bugs," is the most typical change associated with maintenance work. Corrective changes address errors and faults in your software that could affect various areas of your software; design, logic or code. Most commonly, these changes are sprung by bug reports created by users. It is important to note that sometimes problem reports submitted by users are actually enhancements of the system not bugs.

Adaptive Change

Adaptive change is triggered by changes in the environment your software lives in. An adaptive change can be triggered by changes to the operating system, hardware, software dependencies and even organizational business rules and policies. These modifications to the environment can trigger changes within other parts of your software. For example, updating the server, compilers, etc or modifications to shipping carriers and payment processors can affect functionality in your software.

Perfective Change

Perfective changes refers to the evolution of requirements and features in your existing system. As your software gets exposed to users they will think of different ways to expand the system or suggest new features that they would like to see as part of the software, which in turn can become future enhancements to the system. Perfective changes also includes removing features from a system that are *not effective and functional to the end goal of the system*. Surprisingly, 50-55% of most maintenance work is attributed to perfective changes.

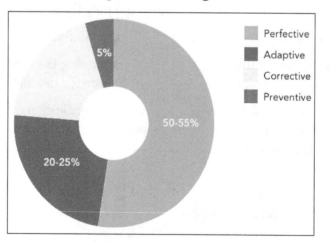

Preventive Change

Preventive changes refer to changes made to increase the understanding and maintainability of your software in the long run. Preventive changes are focused in decreasing the deterioration of your software in the long run. Restructuring, optimizing code and updating documentation are common preventive changes. Executing preventive changes reduces the amount of unpredictable effects a software can have in the long term and helps it become scalable, stable, understandable and maintainable.

How to Maintain Software

The management of software assets has become much more complex since the days when the corporate user had one PC on the corporate LAN running a small number of applications. These days, users employ a range of applications on their PCs, laptops and handheld devices, each requiring support. The complexity is compounded by the increasing number of corporate users working on the road or in remote offices that are beyond the reach of traditional LAN-based management systems. With more systems and more applications in more places, budget-constrained IT departments face a considerable challenge.

In addition to cost and control considerations such as inventory and asset management, or logistical concerns such as technical support, software management is in many ways a security issue. As more people work from remote offices, on the road or from home, IT departments have come to realize that user-initiated configuration changes and out-of-date software on remote machines are the new weakest link in corporate security. The following are four considerations for the simple, secure management of software assets in the enterprise:

1. Discovering and Tracking Software

Simply put, the first step toward the effective management of software is learning what software is deployed. As employees change departments, new people are hired and existing employees leave the company, PCs and other devices are redeployed and loaded with different software versions. As a result, it can be very difficult to track software seat licenses for the purposes of resource deployment and the management of IT spending. Discovering all registered software can help save you money, and identifying unapproved software on a device might save you from a destructive virus or hacker.

Easy does it: The IT staff requires a means of silently and automatically discovering every piece of the hardware on the network, as well as what version of what software is on those devices. Look for a solution that is easy to deploy and integrates easily with your existing infrastructure. Your solution should update information about each system in real time, and enable you to view and assess the needs of groups of devices or users separately from the larger group.

Holding handhelds: Many companies haven't set corporate standards for the types of handheld and mobile devices that are supported. Very often, employees purchase their own devices and are using them to access sensitive corporate data. Discovery of handheld devices is a critical security issue because they are so easily lost or stolen, along with confidential client or corporate information and passwords stored on the device. If you didn't know one of your employees was synching his email to a PDA, you wouldn't know when the person who stole the device does the same. Your asset discovery and management solution must be able to discover a range of mobile devices when they connect to your network through a cradle or wireless access point, as well as identify what software is installed on them.

Keeping things fresh: By having a clear, up-to-date picture of your software assets, your company can be much more nimble in allocating resources for IT infrastructure. Software upgrades, software license purchases and asset obsolescence can be forecast more accurately for future requirements.

How to Improve Software Quality

How you manage software quality has become a vital element of every stage of project management. Are you continually on the lookout for ways to improve your software quality that is not going to break the bank? Excellent software quality will enable cost effectiveness and superior performance to deliver your projects.

Finding ways to implement effective testing strategies at the earliest possible stage will help you detect and solve defects. Solving problems at the earliest stage of project management creates a win-win scenario. Increased efficiency results in better quality software and reduced costs. Conversely, poor software quality exacerbates problems and can become a time-consuming and expensive exercise.

Instead of spending lengthy periods of time fire-fighting software issues, you can concentrate on delivering a quality project. To help you increase efficiency and excellence for your next project we will explain 11 effective methods to improve software quality. These methods are aimed to provide you with assistance so you can deliver your next project with peace of mind in how well your software will operate.

This will help you and your project team take a complete assured approach to software development.

1. Test early and Test often with Automation

To improve software quality, it is absolutely paramount to Test early and Test often. Early testing will ensure that any defects do not snowball into larger, more complicated issues. The bigger the defect, the more expensive it becomes to iron out any issues.

The earlier you get your testers involved, the better. It is recommended to involve testers early in the software design process to ensure that they remain on top of any problems or bugs as they crop up, and before the issues grow exponentially which generally makes it harder to debug.

Testing often requires a focus on early adoption of the right automated testing discipline. Start by automating non UI tests initially then slowly increasing coverage to UI based tests when the product stabilises. If your application utilises Webservices/APIs then automate these tests to ensure all your business rules and logic are tested.

This is an important time to work with your software developers to ensure automated testing is also introduced to your development teams, increasing testing coverage, accuracy and improving quality of the overall product.

A study published in the Journal of Information Technology Management has revealed that the cost to rectify a bug increases roughly 10 times with each passing stage of development.

For Example: An error that costs $100 to rectify in the business requirements stage would cost $1000 to rectify in the system requirements stage, $10,000 in the high-level design stage and $100,000 in the implementation stage.

2. Implement Quality Controls from the Beginning

Testers can monitor quality controls and create awareness in partnership with developers to ensure standards are continually being met. Quality control starts from the beginning, which is an ongoing process throughout the delivery.

A good relationship between testers and developers can help the project software strategy develop effectively. A systematic methodology in quality control can ensure that coding errors and bugs are dealt with effectively, following a structured process.

3. Echo the Importance of Quality Assurance through the Entire Software Development Process

We have identified how important testing is at the beginning of software development; however, the testing does not stop there. Quality assurance should be ever-present throughout the software development process.

Quality Assurance is a governance provided by the project team that instils confidence in the overall software quality. Assurance testing oversees and validates the processes used in order to deliver outcomes have been tracked and are functioning. Testing should be repeated as each development element is applied. Think of it as layering a cake. After every layer is added, the cake should be tasted and tested again.

4. Encourage Innovations

It is important that testing structures and quality measures are in place, however, there should always be room for innovation. A great way to allow for innovation is to automate testing where possible to minimise time spent on controls.

Innovations are so important because they can lead to improvements in software quality that have the capability to transform how projects are delivered. Research and development (R&D) should be encouraged. Empower teams to explore, experiment and investigate continuously. Also, ensure that advancements in innovation are duly rewarded. They have the capacity to transcend your software quality and deliver projects with a competitive advantage over the competition.

5. Communication is key

For any relationship to be successful, whether it's personal or business, communication is key. To improve software quality it is important that all parties to the project have full information through fluid communication channels.

Fluid communication can take many forms. It can be as simple as having clear, consistent KPIs that show how software quality is measured at every step of the development process. It is important that all team members, regardless of seniority have access to KPIs to keep the entire team on the same page. Another important aspect of fluid communication is that all parties have the opportunity to provide feedback to the team to ensure that all expectations are being met.

It is also important to keep all stakeholders in the loop and not isolate team members from the vendors or end user of the software. Isolation can cause rifts and can often mean that the project is delayed or may not deliver on the goals expected by senior management.

6. Plan for a Changeable Environment

Software contains so many variables and is in continuous evolution. It relies on several different external factors such as web browsers, hardware, libraries, and operating systems.

These constant external factors mean that software development must be consistently monitored using checks and balances to certify that it remains in stride with its immediate environment. It is important to acknowledge that software is interdependent on these external factors. Accepting this interdependence means that you can plan ahead. It allows you to have the software quality tested, at each step of the process, against external variables, to see how it holds up. The end result is that you will prevent software dissonance and maintain software quality.

7. Take the Attitude of Creating Products not Projects

This step is a reflection of the attitude of your team. Creating a project indicates to your team that you are producing a finite outcome. However, we are well aware that software is changeable. If you produce a finite outcome, before long the software quality will not stand up against its environment.

Instead, if your team takes the mindset that they are creating a product it is more likely that they will deliver software quality that is adaptable to change and can stand the test of time. Focus on delivering continuous small progressions rather than one final end project and your team will deliver an increase in quality.

8. Have A Risk Register

A risk register is a fantastic management tool to manage risks. A risk register is more synonymous with financial auditing, however it is still a vital element in software development.

A risk register will provide everybody aligned on a software project a list of clearly identified risks and then assess them in regards to the importance of delivering the project. A risk register works well for software quality because its creation actively leads to risk mitigation.

A software development risk register must:

- Describe the risk
- Recognise when the risk was identified
- Acknowledge the chance of the risk occurring and its mitigation
- Understand the severity of the impact of the risk
- Identify who assesses and actions the risk
- Relays the response if the risk materialises
- Gives the status of each risk
- Measures the negative impact of each risk
- Prioritises the risks ranked on probability and gravity

9. Producing software quality requires long-term thinking and strategy

Long-term thinking produces software quality because decisions are made to satisfy lasting issues. Here are the advantages of long-term thinking for producing software quality:

- Doing it right first means you don't have to spend time doing it over.
- Placing as much importance on architecture and design as coding ensures the veracity of your project.
- Creating coding standards with long-term vision eliminates unnecessary mistakes.
- Effective peer review ensures errors are minimised even though it may seem time-consuming at that particular moment.
- Testing often allows you to plan further ahead with certainty that errors and bugs have been fixed.

Project leaders need to ensure that short-term gains and immediate gratification do not compromise long-term strategy. Effective planning will make sure all stakeholders prioritise software quality.

10. Outline your deliverables

From the outset of your project it is imperative that your team outline what they are going to deliver. A clear and concise plan of what the project will deliver helps ensure there is an emphasis on quality from the outset.

It also ensures that budgets, resources, and time are aligned correctly to deliver quality. Without clear deliverables it is likely shortcuts will be taken to meet budgets and deadlines. Ultimately, this will compromise the quality of the software delivered at the end of the project.

11. Review, revise, and remember

Producing software quality is not a coincidence. This is why you must always do the following three things:

- Review – Testing often is a pillar of ensuring software quality. It ensures that standards are continuously met and bugs, errors and distractions can be fixed before they spiral out of control.

- Revise – Study what has worked throughout the software process. Utilise what is working and see if innovation can transcend your software quality even further.

- Remember – When you deliver quality remember what worked well and did not work well. Keep an updated record of both the positives and negatives of any given project and turn to it frequently when you start the next project from scratch.

How to Fix Software Bugs

Step 1. Enter the Bug in your Case Tracking System

At the end of all these steps is a phase where you are tearing your hair out and still haven't gone home, yet. Then you will realize one of two things:

1. You've forgotten some crucial detail about the bug, such as *what it was*, or

2. You could assign this to someone who knows more than you.

A case tracking system will prevent you from losing track of both your current task and any that have been put on the backburner. And if you're part of a team it'll also make it easy to delegate tasks to others and keep all discussion related to a bug in one place.

You should record these three things in each bug report:

1. What the user was doing

2. What they were expecting

3. What happened instead

These will tell you how to recreate the bug. If you can't re-create the bug on demand, then your chances of fixing it will be nil.

Step 2. Google the Error Message

If there is an error message then you're in luck. It might be descriptive enough to tell you exactly what went wrong, or else give you a search query to find the solution on the web somewhere. No luck yet? Then continue to the next step.

Step 3. Identify the Immediate Line of Code Where the Bug Occurs

Error List		
▼ ▾ ⊗ 2 Errors ┊ ❗ 2 Warnings ┊ ⓘ 0 Messages		
Code	Desciption	Project
⊗ CS1002	; expected	ConsoleApplication1
❗ CS0219	The variable 'analyzeThis' is assigned but its value is never used	ConsoleApplication1
⊗ CS0818	Implicitly-typed variables must be initialized	ConsoleApplication1
❗ CS0168	The variable 'iMadeAnError' is declared but never used	ConsoleApplication1
Output Error List		

If it's a crashing bug then try running the program in the IDE with the debugger active and see what line of code it stops on. This isn't necessarily the line that contains the bug, but it will tell you more about the nature of it.

If you can't attach a debugger to the running process, the next technique is to use "tracer bullets", which are just print() statements sprinkled around the code that tell you how far a program's execution has got up to. Print to the console (eg: Console.WriteLine("Reached stage 1"), or printf("Reached stage 1")) or log to a file, starting very granular (one print per method, or major operation), then refining it until you've found the one single operation that the crash or malfunction occurs on.

Step 4. Identify the line of code where the bug actually occurs

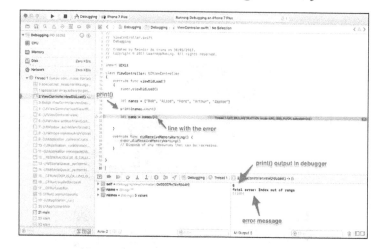

Once you know the immediate line, you can step backwards to find where the actual bug occurs. Only sometimes will you discover that they're both one and the same line of code. Just as often, you'll discover that the crashing line is innocent and that it has been passed bad data from earlier in the stack.

If you were following program execution in a debugger then look at the Stack Trace to find out what the history of the operation was. If it's deep within a function called by another function called by another function, then the stack trace will list each function going all the way back to the origin of program execution (your main()). If the malfunction happened somewhere within the vendor's framework or a third-party library, then for the moment assume the bug is somewhere in your program--for it is far more likely. Look down the stack for the most recent line of code that you wrote, and go there.

Step 5. Identify the Species of Bug

A bug can manifest in many bright and colorful forms, but most are actually all members of a short list of species. Compare your problem to the usual suspects below.

1. Off-By-One

You began a for-loop at 1 instead of 0, or vice-versa. Or you thought `.Count` or `.Length` was the same as the index of the last element. Check the language documentation to see if arrays are 0-based or 1-based. This bug sometimes manifests as an "Index out of range" exception, too

2. Race condition

Your process or thread is expecting a result moments before it's actually ready. Look for the use of "Sleep" statements that pause a program or thread while it waits for something else to get done. Or perhaps it doesn't sleep because on your overpowered and underutilized development machine every query was satisfied in the milliseconds before your next statement executed. In the real world things get delayed and your code needs a way to wait properly for things it depends on to get done. Look into using mutexes, semaphores, or even a completely different way of handling threads and processes

3. Configuration or constants are wrong

Look at configuration files and any constants you have defined. I once spent a 16-hour day in hell trying to figure out why a web site's shopping cart froze at the "Submit Order" stage. It was traced back to a bad value in an /etc/hosts file that prevented the application from resolving the IP address of the mail server, and the app was churning through to a timeout on the code that was trying to email a receipt to the customer

4. Unexpected null

Betcha you got "Value is not initialized to an instance of an object" a few times, right? Make sure you're checking for null references, especially if you're chaining property references together to reach a deeply nested method. Also check for "DbNull" in frameworks that treat a database Null as a special type

5. Bad input

Are you validating input? Did you just try to perform arithmetic when the user gave you a character value?

6. Assignments instead of comparisons

Especially in C-family languages, make sure you didn't do = when you meant to do ==

7. Wrong precision

Using integers instead of decimals, using floats for money values, not having a big-enough integer (are you trying to store values bigger than 2,147,483,647 in a 32-bit integer?). Can also be subtle bugs that occur because your decimal values are getting rounded and a deviation is growing over time (talk to Edward Lorenz about that one)

8. Buffer overflow & Index Out-of-range

The number-one cause of security holes. Are you allocating memory and then trying to insert data larger than the space you've allocated? Likewise, are you trying to address an element that's past the end of an array?

9. Programmer can't do math

You're using a formula that's incorrect. Also check to make sure you didn't use div instead of mod, that you know how to convert a fraction to a decimal, etc.

10. Concatenating numbers and strings

You are expecting to concatenate two strings, but one of the values is a number and the interpreter tries to do arithmetic. Try explicitly casting every value to a string

11. 33 chars in a varchar(32)

On SQL INSERT operations, check the data you're inserting against the types of each column. Some databases throw exceptions (like they're supposed to), and some just truncate and pretend nothing is wrong (like MySQL). A bug that I fixed recently was the result of switching from INSERT statements prepared by concatenating strings to parameterized commands: the programmer forgot to remove the quoting on a string value and it put it two characters over the column size limit. It took ages to spot that bug because we had become blind to those two little quote marks

12. Invalid state

Examples: you tried to perform a query on a closed connection, or you tried to insert a row before its foreign-key dependencies had been inserted

13. Coincidences in the development environment didn't carry over to production

For example: in the contrived data of the development database there was a 1:1 correlation between address ID and order ID and you coded to that assumption, but now the program is in production there are a zillion orders shipping to the same address ID, giving you 1:many matches

If your bug doesn't resemble any of the above, or you aren't able to isolate it to a line of code, you'll have more work to do. Continue to the next step.

Step 6. Use the Process of Elimination

If you can't isolate the bug to any particular line of code, either begin to disable blocks of code (comment them out) until the crash stops happening, or use a unit-testing framework to isolate methods and feed them the same parameters they'd see when you recreate the bug.

If the bug is manifesting in a system of components then begin disabling those components one-by-one, paring down the system to minimal functionality until it begins working again. Now start bringing the components back online, one by one, until the bug manifests itself again. You might now be able to go try going back to Step 3. Otherwise, it's on to the hard stuff.

Step 7. Log Everything and Analyze the Logs

Go through each module or component and add more logging statements. Begin slowly, one module at a time, and analyze the logs until the malfunction occurs again. If the logs don't tell you where or what, then proceed to add more logging statements to more modules.

Your goal is to somehow get back to Step 3 with a better idea of *where* the malfunction is occurring, and it is also the point where you should be considering third-party tools to help you log better.

Step 8. Eliminate the Hardware or Platform as a Cause

Replace RAM, replace hard drives, replace entire servers and workstations. Install the service pack, or *uninstall* the service pack. If the bug goes away then it was either the hardware, operating system or runtime. You might even try this step earlier in the process--per your judgement--as hardware failures frequently masquerade as software dysfunction.

If your program does network I/O then check switches, replace cables, and try the software on a different network.

For shits and giggles, try plugging the hardware into a different power outlet, particularly one on a different breaker or UPS. Sound crazy? Maybe when you're desperate.

Do you get the same bug no matter where you run it? Then it's in the software and the odds are that it's still in your code.

Step 9. Look at the correlations

1. Does the bug always happen at the same time of day? Check scheduled tasks/cron-jobs that happen at that time

2. Does it always coincide with something else, no matter how absurd a connection might seem between the two? Pay attention to everything, and I mean *everything*: does the bug occur when an air-conditioner flips on, for example? Then it might be a power surge doing something funny in the hardware

3. Do the users or machines it affects all have something in common, even if it's a parameter that you otherwise wouldn't think affects the software, like where they're located? (This is how the legendary "500-mile email" bug was discovered)

4. Does the bug occur when another process on the machine eats up a lot of memory or cycles? (I once found a problem with SQL-Server and an annoying "no trusted connection" exception this way)

Step 10. Bring-in Outside Help

Your final step will be to reach out to people who know more than you. By now you should have a vague idea of where the bug is occurring--like in your DBM, or your hardware, or maybe even the compiler. Try posing a question on a relevant support forum before contacting the vendors of these components and paying for a service call.

How to Manage a New Software Implementation

1. Explain the Need

You've made the decision to bring in a software system to your operations. It's new information for staff to learn and integrate into their workflow. Explain the rationale behind it such as the expected ROI, the efficiencies predicted to be gained and any other rationale that will help employees understand the need for the software implementation.

2. Kick off the Project

Establish the team that will be involved in training and rolling out the system. Assign roles and responsibilities and adjust any others that will occur as a result of the new system. Answer any questions team members have and bring them up to speed on any information you learned during the sales process that could be of value to them. Create a software implementation plan with predicted deadlines the company should be aware of.

3. Configure the System

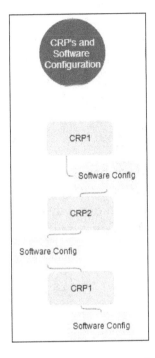

Sometimes software systems require adjustments to match your operations. That's why having team members involved can help work through what needs to occur for the software to work with your operations. Whether it's an integration with other software systems used in your business or custom feature development, time will need to be allocated to account for any configurations. At other times, a software system can't be configured specifically and therefore your business operations may need to be adjusted to match the software tools and the efficiencies they provide.

4. Follow Steps of Change Management Principles

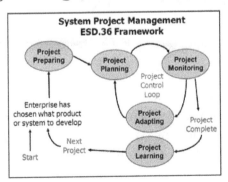

This will help with coordination and implementation of the team and project: Change can be difficult for many staff. You can read more about how to manage your staff through change in our 8 steps for managing through change in ecommerce blog found here.

5. Train

Most software companies will train the key person who will be handling the system. That person becomes the expert or "Power User" and then trains others in the company as needed. If you prefer to train all staff who would be involved at once, then check with the software provider on what training programs and roll outs they offer. Companies will have training documents available that you can use as reference. If there are some specific instructions that need to be developed for staff who may not use the system frequently, developing any training procedures/documents that are reflective of how you want your operations to run is a good starting point to ensure consistency in usage of the system

6. Conduct User Acceptance Testing (UAT)

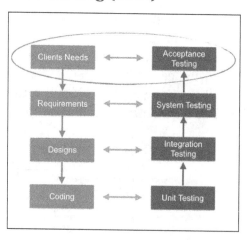

This is an important step to undertake to ensure the software works as intended. It will help find any bugs, (its software, it can happen). That's why it's important to test out a small portion of data to see if the software processes all the information correctly. If the system it integrated with other software tools or marketplaces you will want to ensure that the systems are communicating properly.

7. Coordinate Cut-over

When it's time to begin to move to the new software it's a good idea to keep existing system's information with data still available. For a short period you may be running 2 systems depending on how you decided to roll out the new software. It can take 6-12 months for users to feel fully comfortable with system with a new pieces of software and most times the historical information will need to be accessible. Especially if you are selling online and have returns or warranties to account for.

8. Plan for Go-live

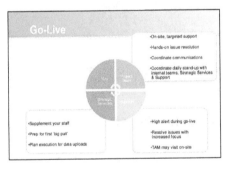

A good idea is to implement a system during slower periods of the year. When companies don't have a slow time, then planning ahead to try to account of any bumps will help. Make sure to have the implementation team ready to work with your software provider on the go-live. Check random pieces of data to see that information and data has transitioned and is processing as it should.

9. Reward the Implementation Team

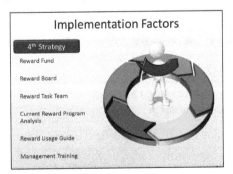

When your team has put in additional work to implement a software system it's a good idea to reward them. Consider having a go-live party for the whole company or provide the implementation team with a little bonus, gift cards and always express verbal "thanks". It can go a long way.

10. Track Efficiencies and Measure Results

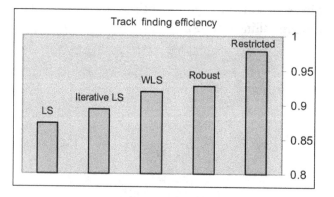

With any system you want to measure the before and after effects. You also want to establish what measures will tell you the implementation has been successful. This can include things like the ability to process more orders in a day, reduction in hourly wages paid out for overtime, or others. Continue to track and measure through the year to make sure your investment is paying off. It's also always nice to see the benefits and be reminded of how far you've come and grown your business.

Software Maintenance Tool

Software maintenance involves modifying the existing software system and recording all the modifications made to it. For this, various maintenance tools are used. One of the commonly used maintenance tool is text editor. This tool creates a copy of the documentation or the code. The key feature of this tool is that it provides a medium to roll back (when required) from the current version of a file to the previous one. Several other tools used in software maintenance are listed in table.

Name	Description
File comparator	Compares two files or systems and maintains the record of the differences in the files. In addition, it determines whether the two files or the systems are identical.
Compiler and linker	Compilers are used to check syntax errors and in some cases, locate the type of errors. When the code is compiled, the linker is used to link the code with other components, which are required for the program execution. Linkers sometimes are used to track the version numbers of the components so that appropriate versions are linked together.
Debugger	Allows tracing the logic of the program and examines the contents of the registers and memory areas.
Cross-reference generator	Assures that the changes in code are in compliance with the existing code. When a change to a requirement is requested, this tool enables to know which other requirements, design, and code components will be affected.
Static code analyzer	Measures information about the code attributes such as the number of lines of code, number of spanning paths, and so on. This can be calculated when the new versions of the system are developed.

How to use Debugger to Debug Software

Take a Look at the Initial Report

This goes without saying, but in order to fix a bug, you first need to have some clue of what the problem is.

If set up correctly, use the form fields below to see the issue's ID, title and description instantly.

Description

Alternatively, go into your project management software and take a look at the user story for the bug report.

Pay attention to any potentially relevant context or attachments (such as screenshots of the issue, or any detailed description of the topic).

Log in to your Code Repository

Now that you have a rough idea of what is going wrong, you'll need to log in to your code repository in order to get a look at the offending code.

Whether you're using GitHub, Bitbucket or ProjectLocker, log into your account and navigate to the relevant project.

Navigate to your Bug Fix Fork

In order to make any changes to your code, you're going to need to access a fork; usually, this is a specific fork which is used only for debugging purposes. Note that, depending on your repository, you may also need to download the fork onto your computer in order to make any changes.

Although the navigation process will vary slightly depending on the repository of your choice, the term "fork" for a copy of the code is pretty universal, so you shouldn't have any issue finding the correct one.

Create a New Branch

The final stage of preparation is to create a branch of the fork to work on your specific bug. This helps when reviewing your bug fixes, as all fixes can be viewed as separate branches, rather than one huge clump.

Again, the repo you are using will alter this step, but we'll use GitHub as a typical example. All you have to do is to navigate to your repo's branch selector menu and type in the name of your new branch. When the branch is not detected through a general search, you will be given the option of creating a new one.

Reproducing the Issue

Replicate the Branch's Conditions

The first active step in debugging your work is reproducing the problem, as this will allow you to focus down on the exact piece of code which is causing the problem. To this end, you need to combine what you have seen from the bug report with your new branch.

Essentially, take any conditions that were mentioned in the original bug report and apply them to the branch. This could be pretty much anything, so work with whatever information you have been given. For example, you could be entering conditions such as:

- A particular user attempting to log in
- Any detailed software configurations
- Widgets being used
- Any set action being carried out

Obviously, there are hundreds and hundreds of potential conditions, but your user story should give you enough concise information that specifying these will not be an issue.

Reproduce the Bug

Now that you've entered the relevant variables, it's time to run your branch and reproduce the bug which has been reported. This will allow you to begin focusing down on the section of code which is causing the issue.

Make sure that you note down your method in the form field below, which can be linked back to the original user story to automatically update it.

Bug Recreation Method

Whilst this step is as easy as running your branch of code with the new conditions and checking for the presence of the bug, its success will entirely depend on the conditions of the previous step - or rather, their validity. During this step, it is also worth noting down any extra bugs you find in a new user story within your project management app.

If the reported bug does not make an appearance, chances are that you need to go back in the software debugging process and alter the conditions of the branch.

Finding the Bug

Insert Initial Breakpoints

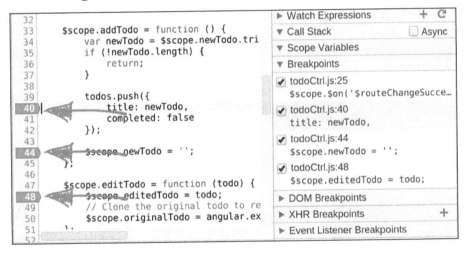

There's no sense in analyzing your entire code repository in order to find a single bug; the sheer number of variables would be unmanageable. Instead, you need to enter breakpoints into your branch so that you can pause and review manageable chunks of data.

Once again, the method for entering these breakpoints varies, depending on the software and code structure you are using. To use Chrome Developer Tools as an example, you can either click the number of the line of code where you wish the breakpoint to be, or you can type the debugger keyword into your code itself.

The location of your breakpoints is pretty much up to you, and will vary greatly depending on the bug in question. If you are certain that a particular feature is causing the issue, a good practice would be to isolate that feature's code with breakpoints.

Analyze your Code with a Debugger

You've reproduced your bug successfully and have breakpoints to split up your data into manageable chunks. Now it's time to break out the debugger itself.

Run through the code with your choice of debugger, examining the variables every step of the way. Line for line (yes, it's tedious, but it works) verify what the program is doing and flag any segments which are not playing along.

There are several techniques which can make this analysis easier, such as:

- Talking to a rubber duck (explaining your code out loud until you cannot explain what a line does; this will likely be a source of the bug)

- Writing technical specifications (examining what should happen against what actually occurs)

- Using test cases (running smaller segments of suspicious code with sets of test variables to check functionality)

Remember to cordon off sections of your code with breakpoints as you go along; if you find that a section is working correctly, put a breakpoint to prevent yourself going over that same segment again.

Keep going until you've found the precise location of the errant code which needs fixing.

Deploying your Fix

Write your solution

Once you have the bug isolated, you can actually work on correcting it. Import your code branch into a text editor of your choice, then get to work on your solution.

Remember to use the form field below to note your fix down.

Bug Fix

Remember that any changes you make are not final; they still need to be checked and put through your software deployment method before going live. Nevertheless, be as thorough as humanly possible - any error you make here will only require your attention later, when the resulting bug from it is reported and slotted into the next sprint.

Once you have completed your fix, note it in the form field below.

Make a Pull Request

99 little bugs in the code.
99 little bugs in the code.
Take one down, patch it around.

127 little bugs in the code...

Once you have identified the bug and drafted the most valid solution, the final step in your software debugging process is to deploy your fix.

How to use File Compare

Steps

1. Open ExamDiff Pro and select the Files option in the Compare dialog.

2. The first way you can choose the files you want to compare is by typing the file paths into the two text boxes. Note that these text boxes use AutoComplete - as you type a file path the program will attempt to complete it.

3. Another way to select the files is by clicking on the a drop-down arrow. The drop-down boxes remember the last 20 files you compared by default, and this number can be changed in Options | Misc.

4. A third way to specify the files is by clicking on the Browse buttons (the ones closest to the text boxes), and then browsing for the files you want.

5. Yet another way to choose the files is through drag-and-drop. Select a file or files from anywhere outside of ExamDiff (preferably from Windows Explorer or some other file management program) and drag them onto the Compare dialog box.

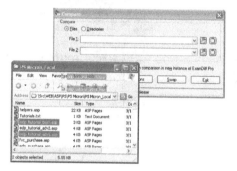

6. Finally, after you have chosen the files to compare, click on the Compare button, and the files will be compared.

How to Clean up a Computer and Fix Problems for Free

The longer you use a computer without performing some basic maintenance, the more sluggish it will become. If you've noticed a significant decrease in your computer's speed lately, or you're trying to get an older computer running smoothly, there are several things you can do. If you're experiencing errors or other issues, the solution may be as simple as rebooting your computer. If you have an adware infection, there are programs designed to scan for and remove these threats.

Part 1. Basic Troubleshooting

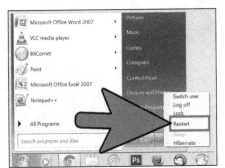

1. Reboot your computer if you're experiencing issues. This may sound like a simple suggestion, but rebooting your computer will solve more problems than you may think. Make sure to save any open documents before rebooting.

2. Reset your network if you can't connect to the internet. If you could visit websites, and now you can't, try rebooting your network hardware. This will often fix connection problems with modems and routers.

- Unplug the power cable from your modem, and unplug the power cable from your router (if you have one).

- Wait about thirty seconds, then plug your modem back in.

- After the lights on your modem have finished turning on, plug your router back in. Your network should be up and running again in about a minute.

3. Check your computer's clock. if your system clock somehow got set incorrectly, you may not be able to load security certificates from websites. This can cause problems loading many webpages. Check your system clock and set it to the correct time.

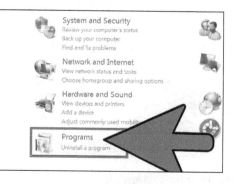

4. Reboot your printer if you can't connect to it. If your printer is no longer appearing, rebooting it may get it to show up again. Either turn the printer off with the Power button or pull the power cord out. Wait about thirty seconds, then power it back on.

Part 2. Removing Adware and Cleaning Browsers (Windows)

1. Open the Control Panel. If your web browsers are running slow, or your plagued with pop-ups, advertisements, and toolbars, you may have an adware infection. Adware is unwanted software that is designed to hijack your web browser, leading you to different searches and littering your browser with ads. The first step towards removing these infections is by uninstalling unknown programs through the Control Panel. The process varies a little depending on your version of Windows:

- Windows 10 and 8 - Right-click on the Windows button and select "Control Panel."

- Windows 7, Vista, and XP - Click the Start button and select "Control Panel" from the Start menu.

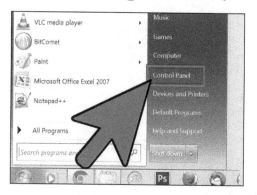

2. Select "Uninstall a program" or "Programs and Features." This will display a list of all of the programs installed on your computer.

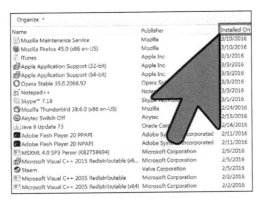

3. Find recently-installed programs that you don't recognize. You can sort the list by install date, which can help you find programs that may have been installed recently without your knowledge. Go through each program on the list and make note of the ones you don't recognize. Perform a web search for each unrecognized entry to determine if it is an unwanted program.

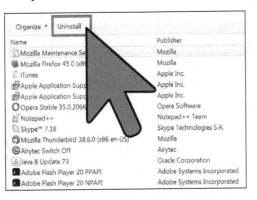

4. Select an unwanted program and click "Uninstall." Follow the prompts to remove the program from your system. Repeat for any additional programs that you want to remove.

- This would be a good time to remove programs that you do recognize, but no longer need. Old games, unused browsers, utilities that you used once and then never used again, and other legitimate programs can add to your computer's bloat. Remove them to free up some space and potentially speed up your computer's start-up time.

5. Download AdwCleaner. This is a free utility that will scan for common adware and malware, and then remove what it finds. You can download AdwCleaner from toolslib.net/downloads/view-download/1-adwcleaner/.

6. Run AdwCleaner. Click the "Scan" button in AdwCleaner to scan your computer for infections. This may take 20 minutes or so to complete. Once the scan is complete, click "Clean" to remove any infections that AdwCleaner found.

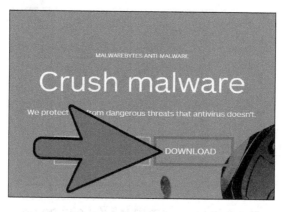

7. Download and install Malwarebytes Anti-Malware. The free version of this program can find and remove most infections. You can download the installer by visiting malwarebytes.org and selecting "Download." You can then click the "Download Free Version" button. Run the installer after downloading it to install the program.

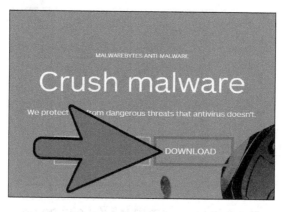

8. Run a scan in Anti-Malware. Launch Malwarebytes Anti-Malware and download any updates if prompted to. Start a scan of your computer, which may take 20-30 minutes. Remove anything that the scan finds by clicking "Quarantine All" after the scan has completed.

Shortcut Cleaner 1.3.9.0

DOWNLOAD NOW
@BleepingComputer

Author:	BleepingComputer
License:	Free
Operating System:	Windows XP/Vista/7/8 32-bit program. Can run o____ ___ 64-bit OS.
Version:	1.3.9.0
File Size:	453 KBs

9. Download and run a shortcut cleaner. Many adware infections will add links to your browser shortcuts, which will cause the wrong website to load even after removing the infection. A free shortcut cleaner created by the anti-malware community can scan all of your shortcuts and remove malicious links. You can download the scanner here. Run the downloaded program to quickly scan and fix your browser shortcuts.

Accessibility

Add additional accessibility features

System

☐ Continue running background apps when Google Chrome is closed

☑ Use hardware acceleration when available

Reset settings

Restore settings to their orig___

Reset settings

Hide advanced settings...

10. Reset your web browsers. Your web browsers may still have lingering remnants of the malware removed by the scanners. Resetting your browsers will remove any additional software and return them to their default settings:

- Internet Explorer - Click the Tools button and select "Internet options." Click the "Advanced" tab and click "Reset." Check the "Delete personal settings" box and click "Reset."

- Chrome - Click the Chrome Menu button and select "Settings." Click "Show advanced settings" and then scroll to the bottom. Click "Reset settings" and then click "Reset."

- Firefox - Click the Firefox Menu button and then click "?". Select "Troubleshooting Information" and then click "Refresh Firefox." Click "Refresh Firefox" again to confirm.

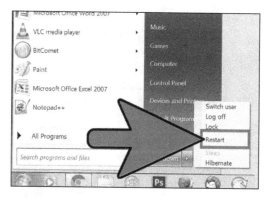

11. Reboot your computer and run Anti-Malware and AdwCleaner again. After you're finished cleaning and resetting your shortcuts and browsers, you should reboot your computer and run both scans again. There may still be lingering traces that show up again after a reboot.

Part 3. Removing Adware and Cleaning Safari (Mac)

1. Remove any unknown programs from your Applications folder. Your Applications folder houses all of the programs that are installed on your system. If you see some suspicious programs that you don't recognize, drag them to the Trash to uninstall them.

- Perform a web search for each program that you don't recognize to see what it does and if it is safe.

2. Download and install Malwarebytes Anti-Malware for Mac. This program used to be called AdwareMedic, and is one of the most effective tools for finding and removing malware on a Mac. You can download the program for free from malwarebytes.org/antimalware/mac/.

- Once you've downloaded the file, double-click it and drag Anti-Malware for Mac into your Applications folder.

- If you get a message saying that you can't install the program since it's not from the App Store, right-click (Ctrl-click) the downloaded file, select "Open," then select "Open" again.

![Malwarebytes Anti-Malware dashboard showing "never been run on your" with a Scan Now button]

3. Launch Anti-Malware for Mac and scan your computer. You'll be prompted for your admin password when you launch Anti-Malware for the first time. This is required in order to remove certain files from protected areas that need special privileges. Click the "Scan" button to begin scanning your Mac for malware. This will take about 15-20 minutes.

4. Click "Remove Selected Items" after the scan is complete. This will remove anything that Anti-Malware finds during the scan. You may be prompted to reboot your computer to complete the process.

Part 4. Optimizing your Computer (Windows)

1. Update Windows. Installing the latest available updates may help fix errors you're experiencing, and will keep your computer secure and stable. Windows Update will handle all of the checking

and installing. Open the Start menu or screen and type "windows update" to find the Windows Update utility.

- In Windows 10, you can find the Windows Update utility in the "Update & Security" section of the new Settings menu.

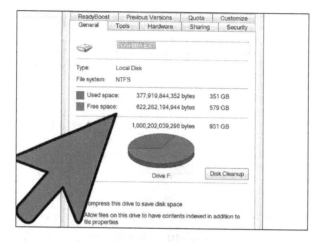

2. Check your available free space. The amount of space on your hard drive doesn't normally have a massive impact on your performance, but if you dip below 20% free space on the drive Windows is installed on, you may notice some slowdown. Windows relies on this free space to move and store temporary files, and without it your computer can slow to a crawl. Regularly clearing out old files can help keep your system running smoothly.

- Open the Computer/This PC window (⊞ Win+E) and find your Windows drive (usually C:). This drive should have at least 20% free space available for optimum performance.

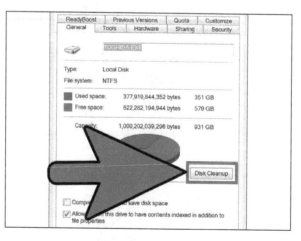

3. Run the Disk Cleanup tool to scan for and remove old temporary files. Open the Start menu or screen and type "disk cleanup" to find the utility. Select your Windows drive and wait for it to be analyzed. Check the boxes for each of the types of files you want to remove. Each entry will display how much space you will reclaim by deleting them.

- Check your Downloads and Documents folders to see if you're stockpiling old files you don't need anymore.

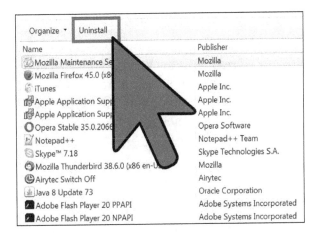

4. Uninstall old, unused programs. As you use your computer, you'll likely accrue a variety of programs that you used once but then forgot about. These old programs can take up a lot of space on your drive, and some may be running in the background, taking up system resources. Regularly uninstalling old programs can help keep your computer running smoothly.

- Open the Control Panel and select "Uninstall a program" or "Programs and Features." Make your way through the list of installed programs and remove the ones you don't use anymore. Highlight a program and click "Uninstall" to remove it. If you aren't sure what a program is, look it up using a web search.

  ◦ A free program called "PC Decrapifier" can scan your computer for software that many people consider unnecessary. These unwanted programs typically come preinstalled on computers, and are referred to as "bloatware." You can download PC Decrapifier for free for home use at pcdecrapifier.com. It doesn't need to be installed, just run the program after downloading it and allow it to scan your computer. If it finds any bloatware, it can remove all of it at once.

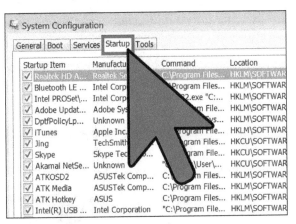

5. Clean up your startup sequence. Many programs will set themselves to start alongside Windows. While this makes opening the program quicker when you need it, too many programs can have a significant impact on the time it takes for Windows to start.

- Windows 10 and 8 - Press Ctrl+⇧ Shift+Esc to open the Task Manager. Click "More details" to expand it, then click the "Startup" tab. Select the items you want to remove from your startup and click "Disable." If you aren't sure what a program is or if its required for start-up, perform a web search for it.

- ○ Windows 7 and Vista - Press ⊞ Win+R and type "msconfig." Click the "Startup" tab. Uncheck the box next to each item you want to disable. If you don't know what one of the programs is, you can look it up online. Just type the "Startup Item" name into a search engine and the first results should let you know what it is.

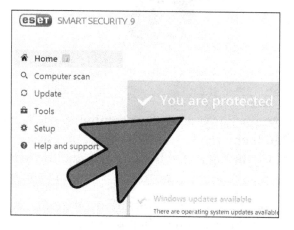

6. Try alternative programs for some of your favorites. A lot of popular programs are poorly opti-mized, and can slow your computer down when they're running. Common culprits include Norton Antivirus, iTunes, and Adobe Reader. All of these programs have free, light-weight alternatives that can significantly speed up your computer.

- • Instead of using Norton as your antivirus, consider using Windows' built-in Microsoft De-fender. Avast and Bit-Defender are also two popular free options. See Turn On Windows Defender for instructions on using Windows Defender.

- • If you use iTunes for your media, consider a program like foobar2000 or MediaMonkey, both of which support syncing your iOS device.

Part 5. Optimizing your Computer (Mac)

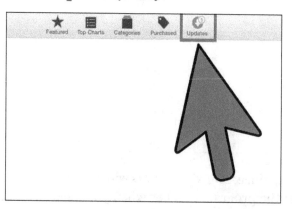

1. Install the latest available updates. Your Mac OS X and other software updates can keep your system stable and running smoothly. Updates should install automatically, but it's good to check every once in a while and see if an essential update is queued.

- Open the Mac App Store and click the Updates tab at the top of the window. Review and install any available updates for your system and installed programs.

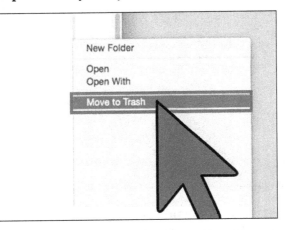

2. Free up space on your hard drive. If you're running low on free space, your Mac's performance may take a hit. Clearing out old files and programs can go a long way towards improving your Mac's responsiveness.

- Uninstall old programs by dragging them from the Applications folder to the Trash.

- Check your Downloads and Documents folders to see if there are any old files that you can delete.

- Programs like CleanMyMac3, Disk Inventory X, and DaisyDisk can find and remove tons of old junk files from your computer. You can free up a significant amount of space using a file removal tool.

- Use Monolingual to remove unused language files. You can get it for free from monolingual.sourceforge.net/. Don't remove the language you use or the English language, as this can cause problems with the operating system.

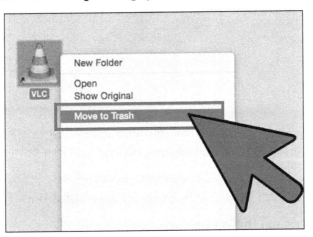

3. Remove excess icons from your desktop. If your desktop is chock full of icons, this could be slowing down your system. Pare down your icons and files on your desktop to help improve performance.

4. Clean up your startup sequence. Some programs will set themselves to start as your Mac boots up. This makes it slightly easier to load the program when you need it, but too many will make your Mac take forever to start.

- Click the Apple menu and select "System Preferences."

- Select the "Users & Groups" option then select "Login Items."

- Select an app that you want to prevent from loading at startup and click the "-" button. You may need to click the padlock and enter your admin password first.

5. Check your hard disk with Disk Utility. Sometimes files and permissions get corrupted, which can cause problems with your Mac. The included Disk Utility can scan for and fix these types of problems.

- Launch Disk Utility from the Utilities folder in the Applications folder.

- Select your hard drive in the left frame.

- Click the "First Aid" tab and then click "Verify Disk." The scan will begin, which may take a while to complete.

- Click the "Repair Disk" button if the scan reports any errors.

Part 6. Keeping your Computer Running Smoothly

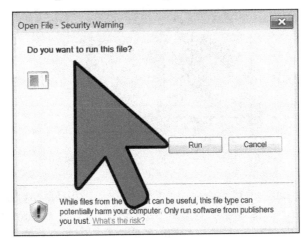

1. Be very careful when downloading programs from the internet. The most common source of adware infections is additional software installed while you thought you were installing something else. Whenever you download a program from the internet, pay close attention to each screen of the installer, especially if it's free. Be sure to decline any additional offers and double-check each checkbox.

- Look for open-source alternatives, which generally will not have any adware in the installer.

- Avoid download sites like CNet or Tucows, as these will try to get you to use their ad-serving download manager programs.

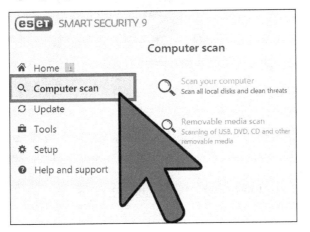

2. Run a lightweight antivirus. If you're using a Windows computer, you should have an antivirus program running at virtually all times. Windows Defender is usually more than sufficient, but you can use Avast, Bit-Defender, Kaspersky, or other reputable antivirus programs as well. Just make sure that you only have one anti-virus enabled at a time, as they can conflict with each other.

- See Install an Antivirus for detailed instructions on finding and installing an antivirus program.

3. Blow out dust on a regular basis. Too much dust can cause heat to build up inside of your computer. If your computer gets too hot, the components will automatically slow down to try to lower the temperature. Keeping your computer clean and cool can help make sure it's always running at peak efficiency. This is even more important if you have pets or smoke in the house.

- You can purchase cans of compressed air or use an air compressor to remove most dust from inside the computer.

- See Clean a PC for tips on cleaning all of the dust out of your computer.

4. Uninstall programs when you're finished with them. If you stay on top of your installed programs, you can keep your computer bloat-free for a long time. Remove programs once you don't need them anymore, and you'll free up lots of space. You can even keep backups of the installers so that you can quickly install them again in the future without having to re-download the files.

How to Keep your Computer up to Date

New upgrades and updates for all different aspects of personal computers are coming out every day, and many of these updates/upgrades could help your computer. But keeping your computer this close to perfection is impractical, so it's easier to do this in smaller steps. Read on for tips on how to keep your computer up to date.

Method 1. Software

Software is basically what you run on your computer. The programs you use to upload pictures from your camera, text editors, and the web browser you are using are all software. Some software needs to be kept up to date through small updates.

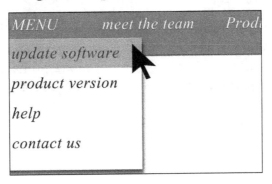

1. Open the program you are updating.

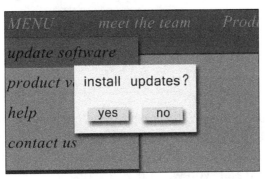

2. Look through the program. Open tabs and menus, and find a button that will install updates (or click the automatic updates box), and allow the updates for the software to install. You don't have to do a full upgrade of software as long as updates are available. However, in some cases, as in Microsoft Office, it may be the better option.

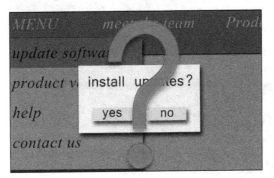

3. Understand what is happening. This isn't essential, just like it isn't essential for a driver to know what is happening under the hood to be able to drive, but it helps to know so that you can enable more options for the best performance. The general idea is that the program is contacting online sources and seeking out new patches for bugs and updates for ease of use, etc. In web browsers, more security measures and better download managers may be given out. In antiviral programs,

more information about viruses may be added to the virus database, etc. For more information about what is being updated, refer to owner's manuals, download details, and the site at which the download is being made.

Method 2. Operating System

Your operating system is also software, but far more powerful and larger than most computer programs. The operating system is basically what your programs will run on. If you are using a computer that boots up depicting the Microsoft logo, you are probably using a Windows operating system. Upgrading your operating system isn't as simple as software or as cheap, but it's well worth it to upgrade it.

1. Download service packs. Before upgrading your operating system to a newer one (or if you have the latest operating system and would like to keep it as up to date as possible) you should download service packs and updates whenever they are available. If you have Automatic Updates enabled, then your computer will alert you when they are ready.

- If you are running a version of Linux, and another version of your distro was just released, you don't need to upgrade to it unless support for your version has been terminated. It can help, but there's no need to go to all the trouble.

2. Be sure your computer is capable of running the new operating system. You should know the specifications of your computer's performance before doing anything related to hardware or software on your computer. Operating systems have minimum requirements for the hardware that it uses. With RAM, be sure to at least double the minimum RAM requirements, and with processor speed, be sure to double, or preferably triple, the required processor speed.

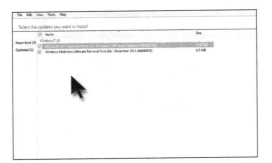

3. Save what you would like to save. This is very important, since everything on the disk will be destroyed in the process of reinstalling the operating system.

4. Install your new operating system.

Method 3. Hardware

Computer hardware is basically the physical part of your computer, the parts you can physically touch. Hardware might include what you are most familiar with, like the monitor, mouse, keyboard, or speakers. Other hardware might be the ethernet/wireless/modem card that gives your computer internet access, or the hard disk that stores your operating system. Upgrading hardware can be both cheap and expensive, depending on what is being upgraded. If it is something like the upgrade from a scroll mouse to an optical mouse, it should be relatively cheap, but a processor upgrade, not so cheap. Don't let this description of prices frighten you when it comes to upgrading, however, because it will be well worth it to upgrade.

1. Research your computer. Find out what are the recommended upgrades for it. Then look into the upgrades you would like. Then find out what is compatible with your system, operating system, and the prices. If you are using a custom built computer, research the motherboard, and what works well with it. Contact tech support forums if necessary.

2. Pick and choose. You don't need to upgrade everything in your computer to be satisfied, but only what will suit your needs. Ask tech support forums what they would recommend for your needs. Remember that you don't always have to do what they say, though, the final decision is yours. Try to be sure that the upgrades will suit your needs, so if you multitask heavily, try upgrading the RAM, if you play games, graphics card, and (if it is a laptop) if you are constantly traveling, the battery, etc.

3. Buy the hardware. You can buy hardware from many computer wholesale sites, the manufacturer of your computer, or at a local computer electronics store.

4. Install the hardware. Take the new hardware out of the box, read all of the instructions. Then disconnect everything from your computer, and open the case. Ground yourself by touching a large piece of metal such as the case itself, then find the hardware being upgraded. Read Build a Computer for specific instructions on how to insert hardware. Once you have finished inserting it, reboot the computer and install the drivers using the CD that came with it, or by following the link that came with the hardware to the drivers. Or, you can contact a professional to install the hardware for you.

How to Find XPath using Firebug

You can find XPath information for website elements using most browsers' developer tools. Firebug for Firefox allows you to copy XPath information directly to your clipboard. For most other browsers, you can find the XPath information for the element in the developer tools, but will have to format it yourself.

Method 1. Using Firefox and Firebug

1. Install Firebug for Firefox. Firebug is a web inspector add-on for Firefox.

- Click the Firefox Menu button (≡) and select "Add-ons."

- Click "Get Add-ons" and then click the "Get more add-ons." button.

- Search for "Firebug" and then click the "Add to Firefox" button next to it.

- Confirm that you want to install Firebug and then restart Firefox when prompted.

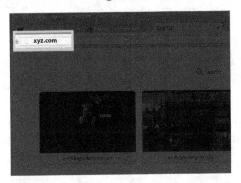

2. Open the website that you want to inspect. You can use Firebug to inspect any element on a website to find the XPath.

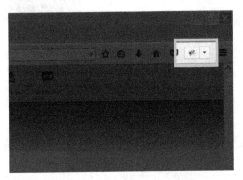

3. Click the Firebug button. You'll find this in the upper-right corner of the window. This will open the Firebug panel at the bottom of the Firefox window.

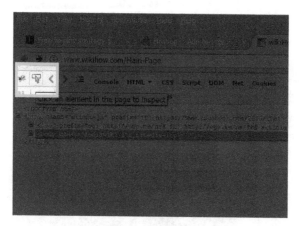

4. Click the element inspector button. You'll find this in the top row of buttons in the Firebug panel at the bottom of the window, directly to the right of the Firebug Options button. It looks like a box with a mouse cursor pointing at it.

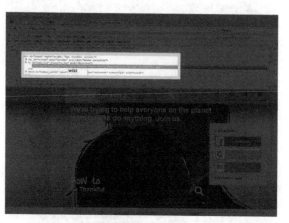

5. Click the web page element that you want to inspect. As you move your cursor over the web page, you'll see different elements get highlighted. Click the one that you want to find the XPath for.

6. Right-click the highlighted code in the Firebug panel. When you click an element in a web page, it's related code will be highlighted in the Firebug panel at the bottom of the window. Right-click this highlighted code.

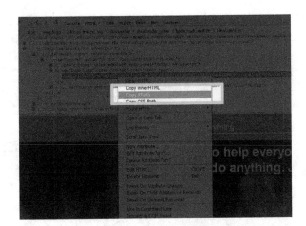

7. Select "Copy XPath" from the menu. This will copy the element's XPath information to your clipboard.

- If you select "Copy Minimal XPath," just the basic XPath information will be copied.

8. Paste the copied XPath information elsewhere. Once the code is copied, you can simply paste it anywhere else you need by right-clicking and selecting "Paste."

Method 2. Using Chrome

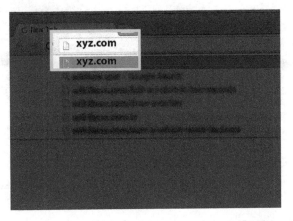

1. Open the website you want to inspect in Chrome. You don't need any extensions installed to be able to find the XPath information of website elements when you're using Chrome.

2. Press .F12 to open the website inspector. This will appear on the right side of the window.

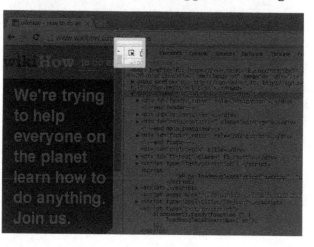

3. Click the element inspector button. You'll find this in the top-left corner of the website inspector panel. The button looks like a box with a mouse cursor pointing at it.

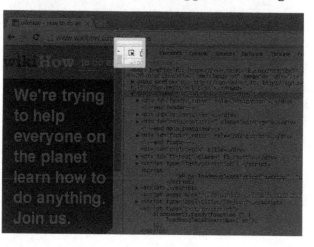

4. Click the element on the website that you want to inspect. You'll see the elements of the site highlight as you move your cursor over them.

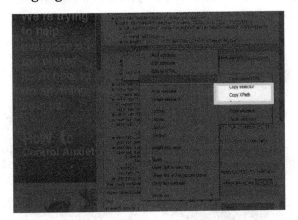

5. Right-click the highlighted code in the inspector panel. When you click an element with the inspector, the relevant code will highlight automatically in the inspector panel on the right side of the window. Right-click the highlighted code.

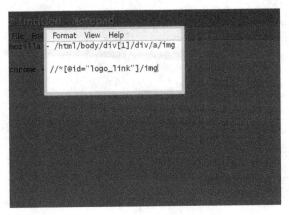

6. Select "Copy" → "Copy XPath." This will copy the element's XPath information to your clipboard.

Note that this just copies the minimal XPath information. Firebug for Firefox can give you the full XPath information.

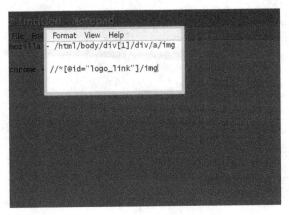

7. Paste the copied XPath information. You can paste your copied XPath information like you would any copied information by right-clicking in a text field and selecting "Paste."

Method 3. Using Safari

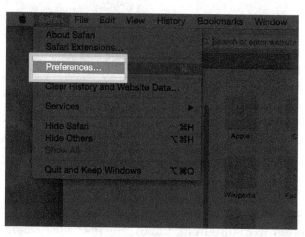

1. Click the Safari menu and select "Preferences." You'll need to enable the Develop menu in order to access the Web Inspector utility.

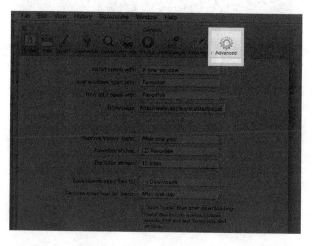

2. Click the "Advanced" tab. This will display advanced Safari settings.

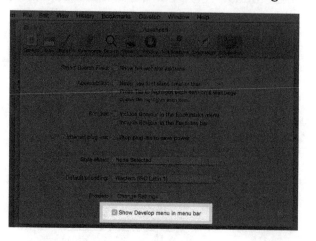

3. Check the "Show Develop menu in menu bar" box. The Develop menu will appear immediately in the menu bar.

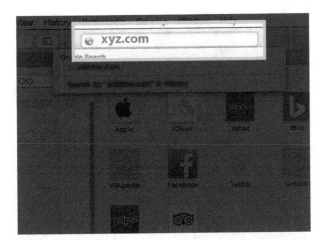

4. Open the website you want to inspect. Close the Preferences menu and visit the website that contains the element that you want to the get XPath for.

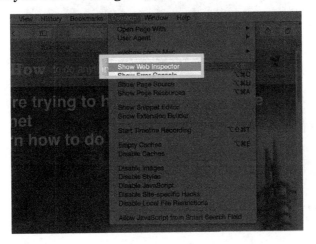

5. Click the Develop menu and select "Show Web Inspector." The Web Inspector panel will appear at the bottom of the window.

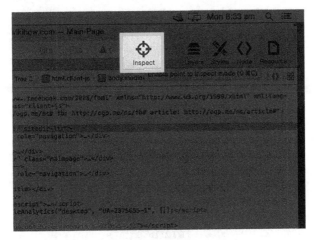

6. Click the "Start element selection" button. It looks like a crosshair, can can be found in the top row of buttons in the Web Inspector panel.

7. Click the element on the website that you want to inspect. This will highlight the code for that element in the Web Inspector panel at the bottom of the window.

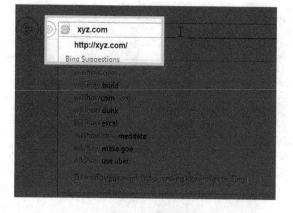

8. Note the XPath information at the top of the tree. You can't directly copy the XPath, but you can see the full path laid out above the code displayed in the Web Inspector. Each tab is a path expression.

Method 4. Using Internet Explorer

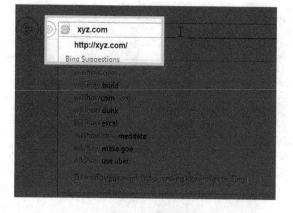

1. Open the website you want to inspect in Internet Explorer. You don't need to install anything to find the XPath in Internet Explorer. Open the website that contains the element you want to inspect.

2. Press F12 to open the developer tools. The developer tools panel will appear at the bottom of the window.

3. Click the "Select element" button. You'll find this in the upper-left corner of the developer tools panel.

4. Click the element on the web page that you want to inspect. This will select it and highlight the code for it in the DOM Explorer.

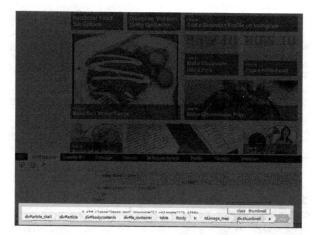

5. Note the XPath information at the bottom of the panel. Each of the tabs along the bottom of the panel is an XPath expression for the element you have selected. You cannot copy it in XPath format like you can in Firefox with Firebug.

Permissions

All chapters in this book are published with permission under the Creative Commons Attribution Share Alike License or equivalent. Every chapter published in this book has been scrutinized by our experts. Their significance has been extensively debated. The topics covered herein carry significant information for a comprehensive understanding. They may even be implemented as practical applications or may be referred to as a beginning point for further studies.

We would like to thank the editorial team for lending their expertise to make the book truly unique. They have played a crucial role in the development of this book. Without their invaluable contributions this book wouldn't have been possible. They have made vital efforts to compile up to date information on the varied aspects of this subject to make this book a valuable addition to the collection of many professionals and students.

This book was conceptualized with the vision of imparting up-to-date and integrated information in this field. To ensure the same, a matchless editorial board was set up. Every individual on the board went through rigorous rounds of assessment to prove their worth. After which they invested a large part of their time researching and compiling the most relevant data for our readers.

The editorial board has been involved in producing this book since its inception. They have spent rigorous hours researching and exploring the diverse topics which have resulted in the successful publishing of this book. They have passed on their knowledge of decades through this book. To expedite this challenging task, the publisher supported the team at every step. A small team of assistant editors was also appointed to further simplify the editing procedure and attain best results for the readers.

Apart from the editorial board, the designing team has also invested a significant amount of their time in understanding the subject and creating the most relevant covers. They scrutinized every image to scout for the most suitable representation of the subject and create an appropriate cover for the book.

The publishing team has been an ardent support to the editorial, designing and production team. Their endless efforts to recruit the best for this project, has resulted in the accomplishment of this book. They are a veteran in the field of academics and their pool of knowledge is as vast as their experience in printing. Their expertise and guidance has proved useful at every step. Their uncompromising quality standards have made this book an exceptional effort. Their encouragement from time to time has been an inspiration for everyone.

The publisher and the editorial board hope that this book will prove to be a valuable piece of knowledge for students, practitioners and scholars across the globe.

Index

Printed in the USA
CPSIA information can be obtained
at www.ICGtesting.com
JSHW060824300124
56243JS00033B/42